RELEASE YOUR INNER

DRAGON

JAMES DRAGONTRAIN

Release Your Inner Dragon
Copyright © 2023 by James Dragontrain

ISBN
978-1-961250-12-3 (Paperback)
978-1-961250-11-6 (eBook)
978-1-961250-13-0 (Hardcover)

DEDICATION

For my sons, Brayden and Riley

May your hearts be the brightest light and a beacon
for others to follow.

TABLE OF CONTENTS

AUTHOR NOTE

Throughout this book you will find potentially life-changing concepts and insights to spark change. This book does not follow rigid traditional formatting to keep the discoveries of information fresh until the end. Keep in mind that, since some of the principles overlap, there is some repetition of information. Clearly, some perspectives are well worth repeating.

I sincerely hope you enjoy this book and realize far more value than you ever expected.

PROLOGUE
THE MISSING LINK

Master your goals by applying the correct mental groundwork and mental fortitude before you take action, as it will greatly improve your chances of attaining the results you desire. As you apply the mental fundamentals that super-successful achievers have been using for centuries, you will discover that *money and success really is mind over matter.*

All the highly successful people you have met or heard about have one thing in common regarding their success as an individual: a *burning desire to succeed.* That cutting-edge focus is not an inherent trait, but a *cultivated fixation* that the beholder feels with every fiber of his or her being. When you meet these individuals in business or any other competitive environment, you are likely to notice that they have a highly defined, focused personality that is targeted on forward movement toward their goals.

Traits such as focus and clarity are key parts of the formula for success, but at your core, your mental self-inhibiting barriers have to be overcome, *when you cultivate a solid belief* that your goal is inevitable, using clarity and focus. Then it is only a matter of time before it happens: your success becomes all but inevitable!

Doing the mental preparation or groundwork creates the mental foundation on which you can and will perpetuate your success, and it is most often the missing link in the success formula.

The sharp mental preparedness, the drive for success, the eye of the tiger can be 100 percent yours if you want it and commit to applying the fundamentals laid out for you in this book.

This information is the culmination of a lifetime of study of the truly amazing human condition and the mental evolution that is happening all around us. Over the years, it became apparent to me that many great speakers and mentors have wonderful, inspirational information to share, but no one in particular is breaking down *success* into personal mental conditioning and the changeable mental template we all have.

We are all conditioning our minds every day. The methodology in this book allows you to control what is going on in your mind so you can reap the unlimited benefits of your potential. This is the difference between success and no change; it is what I call *mind-over-matter thinking*.

Today distractions, competition, daily obligations, fatigue, and mental states cause most people to apply themselves to their goals in a "chip away at it" manner. Without the mental preparedness, the often arduous path to success can become a burden ending in disappointing results.

For most people, making mental paradigm changes is a straightforward process, but it takes time and commitment to change your mental perspective. All of us have spent a lifetime telling ourselves what we believe to be true, and often self-inhibiting thoughts make up a significant part of our belief system, which in turn becomes our limiting reality.

True mental grassroots change changes your life and reality forever.

INTRODUCTION

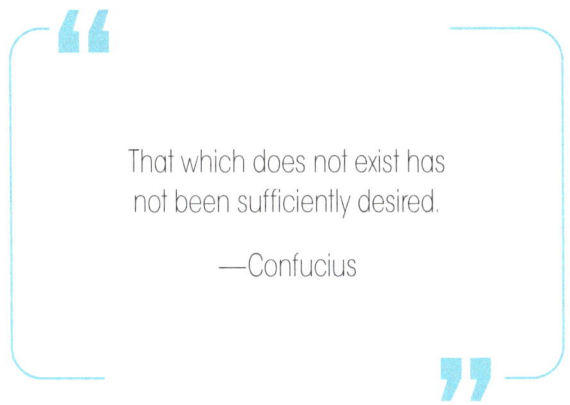

That which does not exist has
not been sufficiently desired.

—Confucius

Change itself starts with the all-important decision to create it. The decision to follow through to a desired goal must not be taken lightly, because it takes time and commitment to be successful.

You also must *see your victory or goal very clearly* and be able to savor the belief and the satisfaction of accomplishment in your mind during the time needed to attain it. Without satisfaction in your mind regarding the end point, there is a good chance you will fall short of your goal. Learning to want it so badly you can taste it is one of the key steps to getting what you want.

Mental preparedness and clarity are key factors. You have to define meticulously what you desire, as clarity brings speed and precision to the action process. Defining every end point detail in your mind enables you to move forward to the desired goal with focus, determination, and confidence you would not otherwise possess. When you create a strong emotional attachment to a goal, such as a victory dance or thrusting the championship cup into the air, you have made *the connection*.

Are you starting to get a sense of this? You can enable your senses in your mind—the sounds, the smells, the rush, *the feel* of attained success; these are mental and visual cues that signal that your accomplishment is lined up. Then and only then have you paved your express lane to success.

Imagine a superstar, such as Wayne Gretzky, day after day conditioning his mind and body relentlessly with positive stimulation, fine-tuning his mental connection with the win and the love of the game until he is one with the process of winning.

When the mind knows nothing else, it can be nothing but.

As you savor this powerful emotional attachment, all of the action items will fall into place as needed as you work your plan backward from this point. (More on this topic later.)

When you have a mind-set, there is no need to talk others into your goals. They can plainly see the confidence and enthusiasm with which you are moving forward, with or without their help. Nothing succeeds like success, because in your mind you have already created it. As you triumphantly bring the desired pieces into place, you will build excitement that reinforces the goal.

Many successful entrepreneurs attest that when others thought they had gone off the deep end, their core beliefs and their mental preparation were what pulled them through. Highly successful inventors such as James Dyson, who created more than five thousand prototypes for his cyclone vacuum cleaner, are driven by a *solid mental belief* that success is only a matter of time in which each failure teaches something valuable and that *failure is required* to get to the next step.

I commend you for stepping into the winners' circle and cultivating a burning desire to succeed, because if it were not for this amazing trait of the human mind, we may all be back in the Stone Age.

Four principles of the mind-over-matter philosophy

1. You get what you think about; what you put in is what you get out.
2. Your current mental state or beliefs are a culmination of your thoughts and conditioning.
3. Beliefs are changeable.

4. When you change your beliefs, your reality changes.

When you understand that there is always more to your mental perspective, whether it relates to your past, present, or future, you are opening up to your full potential.

When you have an awareness of the mental processes that are always present in our minds, you can then facilitate your desired changes.

As ominous as this may sound, all of this is very natural and most of us have been unknowingly limiting ourselves or succeeding using these mind-over-matter principles.

"

Life isn't about finding yourself.
Life's about creating yourself.

—George Bernard Shaw

"

BUILDING PERSPECTIVE

Decide what you really want and commit it to paper. Build a list of all the benefits and features of the desired result. When you rough out a concept, make sure it directly benefits you in some way. Even if the goal is charitable, *the satisfaction is yours.* That's your carrot, your motivation, your end point to build on.

We all use a mental mechanism to get things. We want appliances or furniture for our home, and with some investigation, determination, and clarity, we accomplish this small goal if we stay focused. We want a new car, so we focus on that; we commit to the topic and keep it in the forefront of our mind. Working the topic, chewing it over and over, is what brings clarity to the process. Building excitement and emotional attachment to the end result increases the speed with which the goal comes into being.

The point here is that this process is *a mind-over-matter tool* that can be built up, fine-tuned, and sharpened into a cutting edge to get you nearly anything you want.

You say, "Enough! I am not going to sit on that crappy couch one more day. I'm done." Look at the emotion and the mental determination in that strong statement. The intent is clear, the emotional determination is in place, and the action steps are all but inevitable. In your mind, *it will happen.*

This mini-goal is a great example of mind over matter, because it clearly demonstrates the mental mechanisms of commitment to the belief; the action just flows from there. Can you see how your mindset perpetuates action? The same principles can be applied to larger goals.

Your goal(s) will likely fall into one of these categories:

> ➢ personal, such as fitness, weight loss, travel
> ➢ financial, such as savings, investments
> ➢ material, such as real estate, vehicle, ATV, boat
> ➢ career, such as being a business owner, nurse, biologist
> ➢ recreational, such as being an ice climber, photographer

Your goal can encompass absolutely anything that rocks your world, but whatever it is, make sure it is dear to your heart. Whether it's a PhD or a new home in the country, it can and will be yours if it moves you and you are willing to do whatever it takes to get it. It's not about luck or patience; it's about making that mental connection and defining and refining the result in your mind until you cannot wait to think and talk about the exciting opportunities and how this is going to come about for you.

When you select a goal that is best suited to you, you are much more likely to stick with it and succeed. When selecting a goal, keep these seven points in mind:

1. Goals that fit your natural talents and interests are the best choices; if you love to cook, you will find that field much easier to set goals in than one you do not love. If you are not sure, consider your strengths. What do you do extremely well?
2. Try to determine what is important to you. What do you truly desire: creativity, self-expression, physical fitness, money, prestige, power, perfection, a certain lifestyle, or the personal satisfaction of helping others?
3. Set your goals high. They have to be high enough to give you exactly what you desire and more. If your goal is to work in aviation, what is the pinnacle of success in that field? Is flying an F-35 at supersonic speeds the ultimate goal for you?
4. Make sure your goal has all the facets of your future in balance. For example, you see a well-kept home and a family in your future, so becoming a conflict reporter, a helicopter pilot, or a truck driver may not be the best choice.

5. Be very specific about what you want. Without clearly defined specifics, you are much less likely to act on moving toward your goal.

6. Set a timeline for your goal to happen, because it will force you to act and plan in realistic terms.

7. Research your route to achieving your goal until you know it inside out and backward. When you know everything there is to know about what you want, you are in sync with the process of getting what you want. That is your action plan.

As you define your goal on paper, keep in mind that some goals may be unattainable for you. It's not that you cannot become president of the United States or walk on Mars; humankind has clearly demonstrated that you can do anything if you want it badly enough and stick with it.

What I'm referring to is the emotional attachment. If the end point does not move you emotionally in some way, that goal is not your best choice. You can build up emotional attachment or generate newfound excitement, but if your heart is not truly in it, it is time for a closer evaluation.

Most limiting factors, such as money, education, physical ability, and gender are now a thing of the past. Money is now being made available through the Internet for personal sponsorship and entrepreneurial ventures. Search "crowd sourcing" or go to www.

kickstarter.com and look at the examples of funded people and projects.

If you think a lack of education is inhibiting your dream project, think again. The most brilliant minds in the world are now accessible to you through the Internet. There are communities of people that work for cutting-edge companies, such as Google and Microsoft, who had great ideas and got a piece of the action.

Pitch your ideas and goals to the right people to leverage the intellectual manpower you need to get your dream project off the ground or financing by an angel investor. Search "your topic /forum," that is, small business start-up forums or venture capital forums. If your dream goal is advancing yourself in a given sport, forums are a way to connect to top people and the latest opportunities and technology. Local and worldwide connectivity is now at your fingertips. It's all there waiting for you to commit some time and get a firsthand look at this incredible resource.

As the world moves online, physical disabilities and gender-related issues are no longer a limitation. And universities and colleges are moving online; you no longer have to be there physically to get some degrees. One example is Boston University Distance Education, found at http://www.bu.edu/online/.

A goal can range in size from losing weight to running around the world. In business, a small goal may be to increase sales and a larger strategic goal may be to build an international conglomerate.

For most of us, each day is filled with a series of small goals for accomplishing our daily tasks. Generally, most of us are pacified into a comfortable routine that we find less than stimulating. But excitement is found in a new and desired stimulation, such as a cruise or a fresh romance.

Your desires are the only good catalyst for creating a personal goal. Someone else's goal can become yours through a team or business strategy, but all parties need the mental preparation and clarity to cultivate emotional attachment to that goal.

Most people do not have a problem *selecting* goals; instead, they lack a few fundamentals that prevent the goals from manifesting.

It is important that you make the goal a priority for you. Without focus, dedication, and an emotional attachment to the goal, it is merely wishful thinking. To further illustrate this point, take two similar people with the same goal. Both have the goal of purchasing a new car.

Anne has always gone about life and goals with a wishful-thinking approach. She stops to look at the latest car models but never enters the dealership sales lot. She looks at the models and colors that appeal to her, but she feels that the price of what she wants makes it out of reach. She knows that she will buy a car someday, but for now, it is not possible. Her old car will just have to suffice for another year.

Kim has a very focused and defined approach to her new car. She knows exactly what she wants; she has test-driven everything that appeals to her; and the salespeople know her by name. She knows the model, color, features, financing rate, when the seasonal promotions start, the down payment amount, the costs associated with putting her car on the road, and most importantly, when and where it will happen.

You might think the main reason these women succeed or fail is their very different personalities. But, realistically, Anne could net the same results as Kim with the proper approach to the goal or desired result.

A successful man once said,

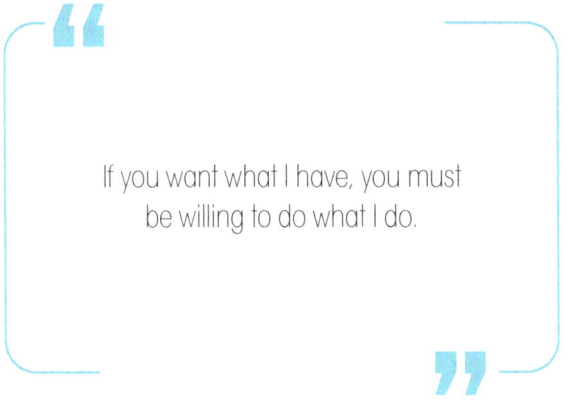

If you want what I have, you must be willing to do what I do.

Reality is either a pain-in-the-ass existence perpetuated by more of the daily grind or it is synchronicity in motion, perpetuating harmony and joy at every turn. Most of us strike it right down the middle somewhere, letting circumstances and influences from people and our environments sway us in one direction or another.

Broken down to its most elemental form, your reality is largely your perspective of the world and your focus on the attributes of your immediate environment.

You and your mental relationship with your world are a culmination of all your thoughts and mental conditions to this point; your perceived reality can be nothing more or less. Think of your reality as being formed and molded by all your thoughts and influences up to this time. The question is can you manifest enough desire to and dedication to modify this state and achieve a desired result?

With this insight can you see why *clarity* is so important? Without daily vigilance and persistence toward a *clear goal*, we are likely to just be ourselves and default back to the thinking patterns of our current realities.

Truly, mind-over-matter thinking is attainable for anyone, given enough cultivation time and determination. You must set an exact definition of the desired change or goal and make a strong, heartfelt, emotional attachment to the end point. By adding clarity to the process through discovery, you modify your beliefs in what is possible. Then and only then have you paved your express lane to your new and improved reality.

"

When you understand that
your thoughts and beliefs are
changeable, you then have
creative control over your future.

"

THE PATH OF LEAST RESISTANCE

The path of least resistance is most definitely the road most traveled. Human nature is to choose comfort and little effort. This is good and bad in my view, because it creates balance but reduces insight or proper perspective for the masses.

On the good side, I see a world that is pacified with entertainment and technology. With world population and metropolitan density ever climbing, without this "path-of-least-resistance effect," there might be civil unrest and competition at a lethal level.

Imagine a race where every living person is motivated to get ahead. Our competitive nature is nowhere near passive; we would likely have everyone stepping all over each other due to the heavy competition. Competition is at an all-time high, and it is still manageable, thankfully.

On the bad side of the path of least resistance, I see talented individuals wasting their gifts. These are people who could easily aspire to greatness but do not want to put in the effort.

The power of conviction is not always summoned from within; often many of the world's greatest minds bear fruit through a willingness to overcome adversity and strife. The middle and upper classes in modern society are spawning new generations of complacent people, whose focus is on entertainment and communication with others, further perpetuating and amplifying the path-of-least-resistance effect.

In my opinion the universe and the world are perfect and balanced as they are; this is the only perspective that allows you peace with your environment. My hope is that, during my time here on this amazing planet, I am given an opportunity to provide insight and to motivate individuals toward their true calling to exponential greatness and expansion of the mind.

"

Everything is perfect in
the universe— even your
desire to improve it.

—Wayne Dyer

"

BE WILLING TO CHANGE YOVUR PERSPECTIVE IF YOU TRULY DESIRE CHANGE

You cannot change your current reality without *moving your focus* off what is happening and what you currently believe to be true. Shifting your perspective doesn't happen overnight. True significant change can be brought about only through a deep desire to change your current reality to an improved state. Your job is to commit as much mental focus as possible to the desire development process and the details of getting what you want.

Your success can be easily undermined by distractions from your current mental conditioning. If you are stating facts about what is and are stating facts about why you cannot be, do, or have, *you are reinforcing your current reality and preventing change.* You must be willing to let go of your current thoughts about what is true. When you believe something is true, it is only a *belief*, a reinforced perspective on your now, on your reality today.

If you are going to be successful at mind-over-matter thinking and achieve the changes you desire, you must reinforce the new desires and the new reality. Lack of focus has the same result as lamenting facts about "what is." Changing your thinking patterns is a process of repetitiously bolstering the desired goal until it becomes a belief in your mind.

You have to want it badly enough that you are consumed by the idea or process. Many inventors, such as Albert Einstein, have been known to "hole up" in their laboratories or workshops for endless hours, to emerge days, weeks, or months later with an amazing prototype, formula, process, or insight.

Keep in the forefront of your mind that negative thought processes inhibit positive change. You cannot use phrase like "I can't because ..." "I wish," "If only," or "that's the way it is." You also cannot listen to negative people who make similar statements. These self-defeating thoughts can and will have a negative impact, promoting doubts and fears, which prevent the building or stringing together of the positive thoughts needed to meet a goal. This process happens long before it has time to take root and manifest in the beholder's mind. I would speculate that no other form of mental self-defeat exists that is responsible for more repressed dreams and goals in human nature.

"

Positive change in your
current reality requires positive
thoughts about your future.

"

SUCCESS IS A FORMED STATE OF MIND

The true meaning of success is based on personal perspective. Success for each individual is defined differently. Your perception of success is likely a result of your environment and the thoughts and beliefs that formed as you were growing up. Your values regarding money, wealth, and success are commonly shared with your parents.

Your parents *or* grandparents were likely raised in a period when money and credit were not readily available. In this very materialistic world, many those from the baby boomer generation and earlier viewed the world from a perspective of lack. In the seventies and eighties, money was freed up, and the "have-not" generations began to make serious financial headway.

Recent transformations in the North American commerce system that have created the "have" generations. Now, in 2013, material items are plentiful and money flows more quickly and abundantly than in any time in recorded history.

From the perspective of the have generations, there is no lack of material items; they embrace prosperity.

Many of the older generations have difficulty relating to the money and to the abundance available today. This is a clear indication that you are living in a truly transformational age of exponential change. Tuning into your *existing* personal success and wealth perspective can be a life-changing experience.

From a species standpoint, you are so evolved and supported by everyone around you that you are already very successful. To change your point of view regarding your personal success "as is" today, stop and think about how you are supported by the evolution of technology and of all the resource and manufacturing industries of the human race. Your health care, clothing, home, transportation, education, and entertainment are the result of generations of advancements that you enjoy *today.* You cannot get dressed in the morning or travel to work without taking advantage of the thousands of amazing human successes you are a part of each and every day of your life.

Each thing you do is supported and backed up by thousands or millions of people around the world. We are all connected. And we need and depend on each other, because we are successful as a unit, an autonomous evolving society. Believe it or not, just by participating you are supporting and perpetuating more advancement for future generations. So if you cannot feel successful as an individual, feel blessed and comforted in the success we all share.

When most people form opinions regarding success, they are comparing their current materialistic and monetary views with those of the rest of the human race. This benchmark does not take into account your personal achievements to this point. To get a better understanding of your personal success to date, list all your personal accomplishments in your entire life. The purpose of this exercise is to help you get a larger sense of your personal success and to improve your sense of success or self-worth. Once your list is complete, take some time to connect with the items. Getting a sense of your past accomplishments can help you project your future goals. List every single thing that made you proud or was a milestone in the history of you. You will likely need to do some outsourcing to collect all the information, such as talking with parents or siblings.

Once you have your list, write down future goals and timelines to get a clear perspective of your personal success to date. The sample worksheet on the following page can help you with your personal perspective regarding success.

My Accomplishments to Date
Elementary and Middle School 1st grade: winner, Mrs. Gerome's spelling bee 3rd grade: Sports Day, three blue ribbons 5th grade: Academic Achievement Award in science 6th grade: award for school volunteer and first place in science fair 7th grade: Sports Day, three blue ribbons, and high academic marks 8th grade: excelled in PE, drama, and mathematics
High School 10th grade: VIP award on the basketball team 12th grade: elected to student council, published articles for the school paper, graduated, and was voted in the school annual as the most likely to run for town council
College Degree in business management, minor in international business management, with emphases in business economics and marketing Nonacademic accomplishments: learned water skiing, downhill skiing, snowboarding, wind surfing, mono-hull sailing

Future Goals

Own my own successful business

Buy a multimillion-dollar oceanfront home with private moorings

Own a sailing and motor yacht

Circumnavigate the globe at least once

Have the financial freedom to travel

Place in the top one hundred in the Hawaii Iron Man Triathlon

Mentor others in their goals

"

The fastest way to success
is to augment your means
or diminish your wants, or to
do both at the same time.

—Earl Nightingale

"

YOUR MIND HAS MORE POWER
THAN YOU KNOW

You have most likely heard it said that we are only beginning to understand the full potential of the human mind. I believe that to be true; there are endless examples of mind-over-matter scenarios, where humans have defied the laws of physics, physical capabilities of the body, and even the diverse metaphysical realms.

People have been known to give up on life and pass away because of a terminal illness diagnosis, while others have defied a diagnosis, decided that it was not going to be their fate—and lived on with a sense of purpose.

Deepak Chopra talks about how a doctor's diagnosis was largely responsible for the fate of his close friend. An X-ray showed a dark spot on his friend's lung. The man had a mental shift and accepted his fate and the doctor's prognosis for survival, and he passed away only months later. After the man's death, it was discovered that the same dark spot was present on an X-ray taken years earlier.

Whatever the potential is of the human mind, it is very large, and we have only begun to tap into it. If you think you can handle a truly mind-altering romp through the mind's potential, read up on Dr. Richard Bartlett and his modality, "Matrix Energetics," or Richard Gordon's Quantum Touch energy healing.

Another mind-over-matter example was documented in the Harvard University study, "Mind-Set Matters: Exercise and the Placebo Effect," which involved eighty-four subjects and their ability to change their bodies through awareness. I love this study because it clearly illustrates two important points: the importance of mindfulness during daily physical activities and that we as an evolving species have only begun to understand untapped mental potential.

Go to http://dash.harvard.edu/bitstream/handle/1/3196007/Langer_ ExcersisePlaceboEffect.pdf?sequence=1 for information on this study.

Or search for the Harvard University study, "Mind-Set Matters: Exercise and the Placebo Effect."

As we break new ground in seeing and understanding our minds' untapped potential, it is hard to imagine what really lies ahead for us. We are only beginning to understand our full natural potential.

We are what we repeatedly
do. Excellence, therefore, is
not an act but a habit.

—Aristotle

MINDFULNESS
IS A POWERFUL TOOL

Mindfulness is another word for awareness—that is, attention to what is happening in the moment you are in. In our culture of overstimulation, we find ourselves coasting or mentally at rest—and rightfully so, because most of us are taxed to the point of exhaustion.

Improved cognitive function lies in adequate rest, exercise, and balanced nutrition, which refuel our minds and bodies, but also in limiting the unneeded mental stimulation in our environment. This will help you put mindfulness to work for you in your daily life.

When we focus on or look for items, people, or situations that we like or are attracted to, these things stand out in our minds. As you *desire, like, or love* things, you make yourself more *aware* of more of the same.

You have used this technique throughout your life when you focused on a subject such as; colors, or types of things, like vehicles, smells, music, and so on. (This is why feminine beauty is so popular in our culture.) Once you have shifted your awareness to these things, it grounds your focus with positive emotions.

As you accept and focus on desired things in your environment, you begin to see these things everywhere, so you have *reinforced your reality and this is what forms your beliefs*, which perpetuates more of the same—that is, what you love about that item or condition.

Unfortunately you can use this powerful tool of mindfulness to bring the things you don't want as well. For example, as you focus on poor health, you will notice that in your environment and gravitate to it.

You see examples of this during episodes of frustration for yourself and others. As they focus and carry on about what they do not like, they reinforce their perspective and perpetuate more of the same through awareness.

> Respond, don't react.
> Listen, don't talk.
> Think, don't assume.

—Raji Lukkoor

YOU GET WHAT
YOU THINK ABOUT

This is why so many people are unable to change their current situation or reality as they say things like "This is as good as it gets for me" or "I never get a break" or "I am overweight" or "It's hard for me to change." In light of this understanding of the process of building and manipulating your reality, how could anything get any better for someone when they believe, expect, and reinforce nothing but their current reality?

Getting clear, positive change is as simple as changing your focus from the things you do not want to what you do want. This shift is a desired conscious process, and you have to want it in order to facilitate it.

"

I cannot always control what
goes on outside But I can always
control what goes on inside.

—Wayne Dyer

"

YOUR MIND HAS A FINITE CAPACITY

Most people only have so much mental capacity. Stimulants such as coffee can extend your hours of focus during your day, but most people overlook an important point for improved mental performance: the mind has a finite capacity for processing information in a given day.

In our high-speed information age, most of us are overstimulated, worn down, and played out due to TV, news, Internet, career information, and frequent input from others. For example, it has been documented in several studies that the average North American metropolitan person is bombarded by over four thousand advertising messages and product information each day. Even if you are a mental athlete in your prime, running on stimulants from sunup to sundown is not sustainable. Even with good rest, exercise, and a willingness to dig in, it is a matter of time before you have worn down and depleted *your most valuable resource*—your mind.

"

Conditioning of your mind is happening all day every day; limiting and allowing in only the stimulation you prefer is the first step toward self-empowerment.

"

YOU CONTROL INPUT INTO YOUR MIND

Filter the *quantity and quality* of incoming information. You can only absorb so much information, so why squander your capacity? I used to be a news junkie. I'd wake up to the news, go to bed after the news, and read everything I could on world and local events. On a slow news day, I could be found looking for something interesting to read on the Internet via my iPhone or laptop. I had no idea how much mental energy I was wasting, and I was clearly not getting any closer to my goals.

One thing is very clear: even if you feel you need excessive amounts of information to keep you stimulated, you are misdirecting valuable energy. Ask yourself, "What do I need to be thinking about to achieve my goals?" If you have stress, depression, fear, or anxiety, you are most likely suffering from improper information input and thought process management.

The components of anxiety, stress, fear, and anger do not exist independently of you in the world. They simply do not exist in the physical world, even though we talk about them as if they do.

—Wayne Dyer

WHAT YOU PUT IN IS WHAT YOU GET OUT

When you fail to manage the information coming into your mind, you reap the negative effects of that information. Your subconscious mind records all stimulation, which is amplified by emotion. So as you allow the volume of unfiltered information to be heard and seen, this becomes part of your mind, part of your mental experience. As you take in horror movies, negative rants from other people, and news about death and destruction, sickness, and disease, you are making that a part of your mind and therefore your experience here on earth.

What do you want your life to be like? Are you currently living the dream or the nightmare? What is your dream for your reality? That's what is important here. Do you long for a soul mate, a wonderful family and home? Or for a six- or seven-figure income? Or do you long to travel around the globe in a beautiful catamaran. Whatever your dream is, it is not likely to come to fruition unless you get your head in the game and focus on what is important to you.

"

Emancipate yourself from
mental slavery; none but
ourselves can free our minds.

—Bob Marley

"

WHERE ARE YOUR THOUGHTS DIRECTED?

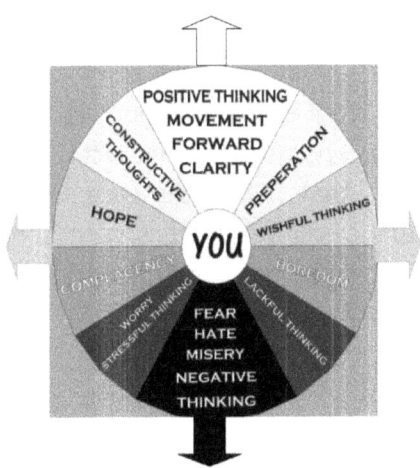

Based on the above diagram, it is pretty clear that where you are directing your thoughts is indeed directional. Clarity and positive thinking are movements forward. Fear and negative thinking are backward thinking and counterproductive. A lack of direction and complacency is your life going sideways or nowhere at all.

Your daily thoughts and spoken words can be very productive or counterproductive in your pursuit of a goal or money, or even in the pursuit of happiness, depending on the direction of your thoughts.

As you bring about awareness to and apply *any* negativity, it creates and reinforces a mental barrier regarding that topic and reemerges immediately when the topic is brought up in the future. In your mind, you are closing or opening doors by telling yourself and others what you believe to be true. Remember this: *a belief is only a series of thoughts you believe to be true.*

If you tell yourself that something like losing weight or buying a new home or winning a competitive event is impossible, that will be the case. Changing your beliefs with the *positive aspects process* is the only way to change without some significant outside help.

"

Everything you are against
weakens you.
Everything you are for
empowers you.

—Wayne Dyer

"

ALL POWER
IS NOW

You cannot change the past, except how you feel about it. Making peace and letting go of the past are the most productive things you can do for your future. Reinforcing what you believe about your past and about yourself only limits what is possible for you.

Your current focus and beliefs about yourself are everything that you are going to have, both now and in your future. Why would you jeopardize that?

When you are mindful of your thoughts, *now and going forward*, regarding what you want and love about your current world/reality, then you gravitate to that. If you can grasp and apply this simple mind-over-matter concept, it can change your perspective and your future reality as you now know it.

You may have heard it said that all power is now. Nothing could be more true. You cannot act in the past or future from your vantage point of today, but you can greatly influence your future through mindfulness and the mind-over-matter process.

"

Always be mindful of your
thoughts and your words, as
thoughts create your beliefs, and
that is the difference between
change and no change for you.

"

MINDFULNESS AND SLOPPY
MIND CONTROL

Funny thing about owning and operating a human mind: most of us operate with very little consideration to our thought processes. Concentration and awareness are second nature to us, and our thoughts process at a breakneck pace. Often we find ourselves ahead of an information stream; we project thoughts and dialogue well beyond a presenter's ability to speak.

Many of us have conditioned their minds to run on autopilot, due to repetitive actions and circumstances. Many of us have driven all the way home from work only to arrive and not remember any of the trip. We thrive on repetition, as it provides a comfort zone that allows us to relax. All too often we get caught with our mind elsewhere when life throws us a curveball we were not expecting. Learning to be present in the moment has many benefits and requires practice, especially when a repetitive action is happening.

Our minds automatically filter out much of repetitive information; many people zone out due to lack of interest and often find themselves asking for help from another when some important information was offered but missed. Some public speakers are about as interesting as watching paint dry; the manner in which the information is presented and the tone of the presenter can make all the difference in the mental participation of the audience.

When your mind is not engaged and you do not let the information in, mentally you were not present. This defeats the purpose of being present physically. I have found myself tired and reading at the end of the day, only to look up from my book and realize I have read the entire chapter and I had no clue what it was about. I hadn't let the information in. Of course, when your mental resources have been depleted, proper rest is the only reasonable solution.

As a side note, I find it fascinating to watch the young, energetic female human mind in action. I find it astonishing how one mind can carry so many thoughts at once and still remain organized and effective, or at least until another female mind appears for personal exchange. This is when the random dialogue can hit speeds than most male minds can achieve only with powerful stimulants or years of practice.

Here are some benefits of staying engaged in a moment:

- ✓ It promotes safety during all actions.
- ✓ It increases individual or group productivity.
- ✓ It complements your physical presence.

✓ It prevents embarrassing moments regarding recall and responses.
✓ It improves response time for any course of action.
✓ It lengthens life.
✓ It improve quality of life.

Sloppy mind control is where no decision or effort has been made to be present or to be aware of the circumstances around you. Being at ease is useful in the proper environment, and it is the hallmark of meditation. Being at ease is entirely different from sloppy or lazy thinking, which is allowing people to think for you and make decisions on your behalf. It's like going to a gym or fitness center and letting someone else do the exercise for you. That would make no sense. Why even be present if you are not engaged in what is going on around you?

Lack of engaged participation is rampant in our metropolitan environments. We now have generations of drone-type individuals operating on minimums. Truly, I think for many people, living the American dream has been a breeding ground for complacency. Never in the history of human evolution have we had so much at our fingertips with so little effort. It's kind of like killing the family dog with kindness, feeding it food and treats until it keels over and dies from overindulgence of the very thing it loves.

Most of us are megaconsumers, fat on all forms of stimulation, food, information, and technology. Many of us need to learn how to have an attitude of gratitude, how to be mindful and thankful for the awe-inspiring times and opportunities in which we live. The amount of doors open to any willing individual is staggering compared to those open to individuals living a hundred years ago.

> "As long as you're going to be thinking anyway, think big.

—Donald Trump

DIAL IN YOUR POWER TO FOCUS

Here's a guideline for *goal-oriented people* who want to limit mind-filling information and entertainment:

- News media: Limit all unnecessary news to a minimum for you.
- TV: Reserve this for wind-down time only.
- TV sports: If this is your goal in life, fine; otherwise, track your hours and/or watch playoffs only.
- Video games: Remove these unless they benefit you in some way.
- Social media: This wastes volumes of precious time; lose this form of entertainment unless it benefits you.
- Newspapers: Read only the best information, avoiding negativity; or get selected information online.

Negative people: Avoid them as much as possible, unless you can turn them in a positive direction.

When you manage incoming stimulation, you make room in your head and your life for the things, people, and goals that you wish to focus on. I highly recommend monitoring each of these areas to better use time and create focus toward your desired goal.

News media can be very negative. Often we don't realize how bad we feel after consuming it or how much the stories affect our day. Many people become desensitized to violence. Most importantly for you, it undermines your focus and intent to move forward in a positive manner. Certainly news can be beneficial, so if you require news, keep what you watch fine-tuned to maximize its usefulness. I love the Internet because I can target exactly what is new and what I need and move on.

Television in general is filler; watching it is a default action when no other choice has been made. When there is no goal or commitment to getting what you want, television provides stimulation. It should be minimized in any setting and used as filler, when no other suitable stimulation or exercise is practical. Unfortunately TV often robs us of much-needed rest, which in causes us to feel unhealthy and to underperform. I often wonder what the world would be like without masses of people pacified into mind-numbing complacency caused by television exposure. Don't get me wrong; I enjoy movies and learning about the wonders of our world and everything in it. I just think it's gone past the point of entertainment and education for most people, especially if it inhibits their ability to get off the couch and get engaged in real-life stimulation.

TV sports are just entertainment unless you are in that field. If you are a successful athlete, sports TV is likely a useful tool. If TV sports are your obsession and you like to sacrifice the time from other more productive endeavors, that is your prerogative. If you are reading this book looking for insight to get ahead, you may want to review how much time you are committing to this entertainment. Sports are all about being the best, and I salute the men and women at the top of their game, but I'll bet they didn't get there by obsessively watching others on TV.

Video games are a quick time filler and are reasonable entertainment when used in this manner. Things get out of balance when large blocks of time are consumed, which can detract from daily and long-term goals, exercise, and constructive activities.

Social media such as Facebook and Twitter can add social variety and communication for people separated by distance. At the end of the day, it is mainly entertainment and a filler unless used as a tool to follow someone's success, which in turn helps you define what is needed on your path to success.

Newspapers and other printed media can consume large blocks of personal time if not properly managed. I recommend reading only relevant and needed information.

Note: Almost everyone enjoys leisure time, and if you truly enjoy a time-consuming relaxing activity such as this, then by all means, enjoy your indulgence. But keep in mind that time is very valuable and should never be intentionally wasted. On the other hand, savoring the moments adds quality to life.

Negative people can and will drain your energy. By venting negative feelings, using derogatory remarks, or telling negative stories, they unknowingly trap themselves in a depressed pattern that prevents positive movement forward. There are always exceptions to this; for example, such as individuals with authority are employed for these qualities to oversee a disgruntled workforce. Surprisingly, these types of people can find a place to fit in with society, but generally they suck your energy and inhibit your growth. People who are negative but don't realize it can change if awareness and desire are present. If this is someone you care about, try to help him or her shift focus to positive aspects of life and opportunities.

"

What you are looking for
is what is looking.

—St. Francis of Assisi

"

MENTAL BLOCKS

The human mind is our biggest asset, and yet it remains our biggest challenge to control. The implications of human diversity and environmental conditioning are limitless. As we push the envelope on every scientific frontier simultaneously, we find ourselves taxed and challenged with the environment we have created. It is little wonder that many find themselves burned out and disillusioned by the pace of forced change.

There is hope for the many that hold on to the belief that if there is a will there is a way. Here is a key concept that, when fully understood, can change your life:

> A core belief about yourself or your ability is only a series of thoughts you believe to be true.

Sounds simple, right? The second part is this:

"

> If you repeat and focus on a new thought enough times, you will begin to believe that it is possible. Given enough time, it will become a core belief.

"

Everything you believe today is the result of repetition or exposure until you believed it to be true. Your thoughts are totally malleable or upgradeable into the beliefs that will bring you exactly what you want in this lifetime.

What this really breaks down to is that you have creative control over your beliefs. Amazingly, this simple fact or tool is not widely understood or intentionally utilized today.

Using repetition and reinforcement about desired results or goals combined with emotion is the key to long-term changes in your life.

In the upcoming pages I have an explanation of the positive aspects process, which is the key to implementing this mind-over-matter change process. This process has both a positive and a negative side. It is nice to know what has been holding us back; most of us have been unknowingly implementing a self-inhibiting thought process that prevents each of us from getting what we want. When you speak a negative statement to yourself and your environment, you are setting up your beliefs about that topic.

Unfortunately we humans, conditioned the way we are, have a tendency to reinforce and believe the negative. Negativity is most often attached to emotion, which is very powerful. Your subconscious mind is like a highly sensitivity video recorder always giving you back exactly what you put into it.

When you describe what you think is true or feel bad about, you record that information. When you add emotion to that recording, it's like hitting the high-definition button. That intense feeling is vividly recorded for next time the subject comes up, so you feel the live results of what you heard, saw, and felt.

There are endless examples of this. My son, Riley, has struggled with this most of his adolescent life due to his highly sensitive nature. When things did not go right or he was criticized by others, he took an emotional hit, and that feeling was recorded deep within him.

Mentally storing those incidents repeatedly left him struggling for confidence and self-esteem, even when he also had positive support. The issue was that the positive information did not carry the emotional component and did not stay or resonate with Riley over the long term. Responding to others with ready-made knee-jerk responses as a defense mechanism did offer him some protection, but often escalated the conflict in the situation. In his youth Riley found himself as a defensive, often distant person unintentionally focusing on negative dialogue and deflecting blame to others. Today, as Riley nears the end of eighth grade, the positive reinforcement has deep roots as well. He still has emotional attacks as he fights to control his beliefs about what he is feeling and what is happening. Some people have a lifelong struggle to get emotionally balanced. For Riley and the rest of us, sensitivity can be managed and channeled into positive productive actions if the awareness and the desires are present.

When we control what we are thinking and, more importantly, how we respond to a highly emotional situation, we are tempering our character, stabilizing our inner being. Once we have mastered our emotions and the thoughts tied to those emotions, we are then grounded and find life to be much more fulfilling and enjoyable. All personal power comes from within, so be mindful of emotional components or emotional aspects during interactions with others. Your responses to others should never be based solely on emotion.

I love Riley with all my heart, for he has taught me so much.

What we think determines
what happens to us, so if we
want to change our lives, we
need to stretch our minds.

—Wayne Dyer

CREDIT OR BLAME FOR YOUR FAILURE OR SUCCESS TAKES AWAY YOUR PERSONAL POWER

You cannot move forward with any significant mind-over-matter changes when you blame or give credit to others rather than to yourself. (Only you can change you mentally.) You can be unknowingly giving away your personal power, but realizing this fact can return creative control to you.

Listen to yourself. If you are saying any of the following statements, it may be necessary to reorient your thoughts using a positive aspects process. You alone are responsible for what is going on inside your head.

- I don't/can't/won't because he or she...
- I want to but.../I would but.../I could but I'm obligated to...
- I'm not allowed to ./He or she won't let me...
- He or she would never agree/would be upset/ would be disappointed.
- I don't know how, because she...
- That's not my problem, because he/she .
- My government won't help.
- My circumstances prevent me from...

When you take steps on the path toward your personal goals, listening to yourself *empowers you.* The satisfaction, the glory, or failure is on our shoulders, and most of us would not have it any other way. The personal pride, self-esteem, rewards, and friendship that come with the journey are yours, but you will not realize it if you give your power to others.

"

Be mindful of what you are
telling yourself about *anything*.

"

COMPARE WITH
GRATITUDE OR NOT AT ALL

Comparing yourself to others can be productive or counterproductive, depending on your perspective. When you look at someone's success or material possessions with praise, you can open your thoughts through appreciation and approval. As you build your desires and goals, you build your personal excitement and gravitate to that.

When you look at someone's success or material possessions with jealousy or contempt, you create emotional barriers to having those things. The process in your subconscious mind works both ways.

It may be hard for some people to believe, but you are a totally self-perpetuating or self-inhibiting being. You alone dictate your success. That is great information for most people. But if you gravitate toward criticism, ridicule, or condemnation, you are hurting *you*. If you are influencing others or impressionable children into similar ways of thinking, you are causing limitations in their future as well.

Think about what this means for you: as you criticize people who are wealthy or healthy or have amazing material possessions, you are creating barriers between you and having those things.

"

If you don't like something,
change it.
If you can't change it,
change your attitude.

—Maya Angelou

"

MENTAL SELF-TALK AND SELF-WORTH

Did you know that your self-talk and self-worth can be seen in your physical appearance? Look in the mirror. What do you see? It's probably not what you see, but what you think others see.

Think of this for a moment: you know of some people who have spent a lifetime listening to themselves or other people talk negatively. These people are easy to spot; their low self-esteem is reflected in wearing clothes that further depict the look. Physical traits may include poor body language, little eye contact, slouching, and so on.

As you tell yourself what is possible or what you think is true, you reinforce this picture or notion in your mind, and it becomes your default thought or perspective. Do you get this? This becomes your reality!

When you think thoughts or self-talk about anything regarding self-worth, it is recorded in your subconscious mind and reinforces your beliefs—essentially creating your reality.

It's just that simple. Never ever say anything to yourself that is negative or self-inhibiting! Below is a list of phrases you should try not say out loud—and never say in your mind. When you say the words to yourself or aloud, notice how they make you feel.

Negative self-talk	Positive self-talk
• I don't deserve this.	• I deserve this.
• I'll be happy when...	• It's going to be great
• I could never...	• I could always...
• Why me?	• Why not me?
• I wish...	• I believe I am...
• Like that could happen.	• That would be awesome.
• With my luck...	• I expect great results.
• I am always sick.	• My vitality keeps me strong.
• Everyone is to blame.	• I love my confidence.
• This is above me.	• I can do this.
• I don't believe.	• I believe.
• I have doubts.	• This is my moment.

When you reinforce your mind with positive self-worth information, you strengthen and correct physical and psychological shortfalls. You boost your confidence; your appearance changes because you feel more confident about yourself; and, best of all, your world changes. People like to hear upbeat thoughts from confident people, and your newfound persona perpetuates your focus on your goal.

Carry a small notebook or electronic device and write down any negative self-talk when it happens. Make corrections by changing any self-talk from negative to positive. Chances are, you are about to discover you are not as positive as you think you are. Start telling everyone an improved perspective about you and your world and everything in it. As a reward for your efforts, watch the positive changes take place. Nothing could be more uplifting or joyful.

"
Self-worth comes from one thing—
thinking that you are worthy.

—Wayne Dyer

"

GREEN
LIGHTS

See your life as a series of green lights. As you move through your day, appreciate the events and the things that work out for you. Believing that positive sequences and events generally line up and showing appreciation brings a feeling of well-being. This is very important to do if you're not doing it already.

Life is not meant to be hard. Looking for positive aspects of your life and consciously appreciating events perpetuates more of the same. Mentally note the synchronicity or alignment of like-thinking minds, and enjoy the good feelings that come with appreciation of your day. When you get in the habit of appreciating positive aspects of your day, you start to have more days that line up with your good intentions and good feelings—until you begin to have good weeks and then good months and good years.

When you believe life is supposed to have mainly green lights, it allows you to flow through traffic with minimal effort. When your focus is on problems or negative things, it slows down your progress until you make little headway and things feel like a struggle. Keeping the big picture in mind allows you to see to the end of the task. Appreciating the benchmarks and milestones allows you to maintain a positive perspective, essentially giving you a feeling of green lights or positive flow and momentum. When you expect a green traffic light, that's what you usually see, and it makes you feel good; when you come to a red light, you look beyond it, telling yourself that you rarely have to wait long and that the red lights are few and far between.

This attitude of gratitude lifts negative feeling off your shoulders and allows you to feel good about your day. Reinforcing positive emotion should be done all day every day, so when you encounter an individual who does not have a positive attitude, your mental preparedness allows you to move beyond that person and his or her problems by protecting you from absorbing or buying into that person's negative energy.

Imagine if you had to stop and wait for every traffic light to change green on an extended trip across a large city. Now imagine every traffic light could turn green for you as you arrive at each intersection. When you line up your positive thoughts, your life begins to flow with speed and efficiency. When you learn to expect it, opportunities and positive relationships will line up for you. It is the same for all mind- over-matter thinking; perpetuating success, money, or relationships depends on you and your attitude toward change.

There is always a negative side to the equation. When you focus on restrictions, negative results and problems realistic or implied will only bring you more of the same, if you believe that is inevitable for you. If you believe red lights are everywhere, then that will be your reality. Use the positive aspects process to list all the good things about any situation that you wish to change.

Affirming all the good things about a person, place, or situation will help you move beyond or through the obstacle. Improving clarity about your desired positive outcome and connecting with that mentally will change your focus and start to perpetuate positive change and green lights.

Persistence and determination alone are omnipotent.

—Calvin Coolidge

Here is an example of making a shift into green light thinking: John always seemed to be late for everything. Often he couldn't find his car keys, or a pressing issue had his attention until the last moment before he had to dash across town or the island, Maui. He knew he was going to be late. Though he always traveled the quickest routes, inevitably there was a delay. He just expected traffic to slow due an unseen force or obstacle, and he instinctively knew that green lights and parking spaces were never present, especially when he needed them most.

Then one day he decided that he had to *shift* his thinking and his perspective to get what he desired. He realized that he had always been focused on results that were the opposite of what he truly desired. He decided to change his focus to the *desired result* of the actions he was trying to accomplish—in this case, being on time. For this to happen, he needed to apply mindfulness and positive thoughts about the process before, during, and after the actual event.

John knew he had an important appointment coming up at around on Wednesday, the last day of the month. A businessperson was arriving on the ferry from Hawaii to discuss a final transaction and sign some papers. This was the perfect opportunity to shift his thinking and get the results he desired, because he knew he had the time to change his mind-set. John knew that crossing town at this time of day was problematic, even without unforeseen circumstances, so his intent was to keep his focus off the traffic and on the positive aspects of the trip. He broke down the good aspects of the trip:

1. First he created a feeling of good will toward the event by looking forward to the journey as a welcome, positive change that he would enjoy.

2. Then he imagined he would locate his keys after he got dressed on the morning of the appointment day. He would feel the satisfaction of knowing he could jingle them in his pocket in anticipation of making the trip. It would be a very good feeling to know the keys were exactly where he needed them to be.

3. John pictured himself being aware of the time on the afternoon of the appointment and letting incoming calls go to voicemail. And he envisioned appreciating that the phone did not ring at all.

4. Next he imagined arriving early at the ferry terminal, strolling down the beach, and watching the ferry come in. He imagined the water, waves, sand, and endless horizon, which seemed to reach out into infinity. He would have time to collect his thoughts and cool himself with the sea breeze that was always present.

5. The trip itself was going to be enjoyable; it was an opportunity to take in more of the very things he loved about the island and why he moved there in the first place.

6. His pleasure in the journey was going to be crowned with a very enthusiastic, positive meeting. Just thinking of the meeting in those terms excited him and made him wish the event was sooner.

7. The trip would be about symmetry and flow. He visualized having mainly green lights. He

knew when the lights were not green when he arrived, he would not have to wait very long. He pictured himself enjoying the flow—and the confidence because of the extra time he would have.

8. Parking was not going to be a problem; really, he enjoyed having someone leave a parking spot just as he arrived. He preferred a shady spot with good access to the grassy areas. Yes, this was going to be perfect.

9. He imagined the type of flawless, sunny afternoon Maui is famous for. He was grateful for this, and he could feel his blessing and good fortune in living in such a beautiful place.

John visited his list in his mind until he knew each positive aspect by heart. Each time he went through the exercise and experienced the positive emotions associated with the trip, those emotions became more real, stronger, and more heartfelt. By the end of the first week, he truly believed the synchronicity was now in his favor for this trip and that this exercise would bring the shift he desired.

Within fourteen days of completing this exercise at least once daily, he began to notice the shift every time he drove somewhere. Each time he came to an intersection, he offered appreciation for the good feelings that the green light provided. The green lights became a highlight of the day, like a repetitive positive affirmation, which in turn caused more good feelings and seemed to attract more positive events and communication with others.

John noticed he no longer minded waiting at traffic lights, because the time spent at a stop felt so short. He began to enjoy trips in his car more and began to believe that a perfect parking spot was going to become available at any moment.

When the appointment day came, there was no question as to what was going to happen; the day flowed into evening and became one of the most joyous days on the island, because he knew in his heart that he had truly changed. It was simply mind over matter.

"

Waiting for someone to change
so that you can be happy is like
waiting for an unsummoned taxi to
take you to where you already are.

"

ALWAYS SET YOUR MENTAL INTENT

Setting your mind regarding your desired end point before you take action is likely much more important than you know. Your mental perspective while performing any task greatly affects the result and how well the performance flows. When you visualize exactly what you want to happen and break the process down, you have a distinct advantage over those who have not made a clear distinction regarding the end result.

When you consider the multitude of human emotions and apply them to the physical tasks process, it is amazing how varied the results can be. It is not hard to visualize a person performing a task out of frustration or anger and the sequence of action-related problems leading to the end result. But subtler emotions also have a significant bearing on the outcome of a task process. If the intended action is a road trip, encouraging feelings of safety and of arriving rested and on time are good examples of positive intent for a trip. If you do not feel safe before taking a trip, mental preparation and closer examination is needed.

For example, during a planning session regarding an upcoming Florida vacation with my family, some anxiety was expressed by the family members regarding traveling unfamiliar interstates at high rates of speed in an unfamiliar rental vehicle. We have all heard stories of tourists having serious automobile accidents. Fear and anxiety because of such stories can grow with time and could manifest with catastrophic consequences if left unchecked.

With my understanding of cause and effect and mind-over-matter issues, the solution for this family seemed pretty clear. In that very meeting six months before the trip, I asked everyone how they would feel if we rented a Hummer for our jaunt through Florida. The general comments were "that would be amazing" and "that would be so cool!" I asked, "Would you *feel* safe?" The answer was "Yes, of course" In that instant, the attitude was feeling changed from fear or worry to ease, comfort, and create positive expectation toward the trip.

Because the new plan was to rent the safest vehicle that we could afford at that time, we could visualize traveling in safety and comfort, which prevented fears from manifesting before the trip took place. When the trip did happen, everything went as planned, and we enjoyed a worry-free trip.

When you have fears or anxieties about anything before an action sequence, corrections are needed— and long before the action takes place. Having a mind-set regarding disaster actually draws you into that sequence. I spend much of my time on the road, so I have purchased the safest vehicle I can afford.

When I set out on an extended road trip during questionable winter weather, I shift my thoughts from worry to thoughts about my vehicle's excellent safety features and its ability to maintain traction, allowing me to arrive safely. By setting this intent and staying mindful of all road conditions and other drivers, I arrive safe and sound every time. You may say, "What is new about this information?" It is simply this: good preparation, the clear mental intent of safety, and the manifestation of good feelings affect the outcome.

Clearly, if I did not have the willingness to shift the feelings or mindset to that of safety from a mind-set worry, I would be setting myself up for whatever comes along. *Always be willing to take whatever actions necessary to make the mental shift.* That feeling of unrest or worry is your cue that something is not right and better preparation is needed. Worry about all the bad things that could happen draws those circumstances to you through cause and effect. Remember, life is like a mirror: what you put out in the form of thoughts and emotion is what you get back.

During my travels, I often see drivers that were not so fortunate and I know that they had not prepared mentally. When someone shares fear-based stories about traveling during winter conditions, I do not share in the fear emotion. I gently add encourage upgrades to make them feel safe while traveling.

Can you see how mental preparation plays a large part in the outcome of any action sequence?

Here is a competitive example of mental preparation. Three people were in competition to perform a sequence of tasks for a given outcome, to be judged by the end result.

Contestant 1 is not very well prepared but is overconfident due to a previous experience with similar tasks. This person has organizational skills, but has been known to cut corners.

Contestant 2 knows exactly what to do but does not work well under pressure. This person fears criticism and has been dreading the competition for some time.

Contestant 3 has been looking forward to the opportunity to compete. This person has practiced similar sequences of events both physically and mentally, has researched winning combinations, and knows exactly what the judges are looking for.

Naturally, investigation, practice, and mind-set won the day for contestant 3.

Mental preparation is a key part of any successful action sequence for your future. Mental and physical preparedness with an eye on the end result is an unbeatable combination. Acting without significant forethought opens you up to varied results due to unforeseen circumstances. But regardless whether you're taking a road trip, going to a meeting, preparing to make a phone call, baking a cake, building a shed or a skyscraper, mind-over-matter mental preparation is needed regarding the intent and the end result.

Gratitude unlocks the fullness of life. It turns what we have into enough and more. It turns denial into acceptance, chaos into order, confusion into clarity. ... It turns problems into gifts, failures into success, the unexpected into perfect timing, and mistakes into important events. Gratitude makes sense of our past, brings peace for today, and creates a vision for tomorrow.

—Melody Beattie

WORDS AND
IDEALS IMPRINT THE MIND

When you use words or euphemisms negatively, they have lasting effects on the mind and undermine your intention. Words attached to emotion can leave lifelong emotional scars in our children and youth.

Phrases such as *you are* and *you will never be* reinforce the opposite of what is intended in the mind for the recipient. Thankfully, the old- school thinking is changing; mostly gone are the days of oppression and forced conformity. Nurturing the impressionable human mind and turning criticism into encouragement is a simple transition that all parents, caregivers, and leaders need to embrace.

Many adults were mistreated or abused as children and have difficulty with their own children. I have seen examples of one bad apple affecting three generations of behavior issues. When you encourage anyone with good feelings and lead by example, you can shift the atmosphere in the home or work environment from negative to positive. Here are some examples of positive reinforcements to replace negative ones.

- You are better than this. Let me help you to set things straight.
- This is beneath you. It happened to me once.
- You always excel at this, so let me help you do better. Let me help you get this figured out.
- You are maturing nicely, and I want you to know this issue really needs your attention.
- You are very talented, and you need to focus on the end result to get what you want.
- Your participation in helping with family duties brings balance and harmony to the whole, and we always appreciate your help. Let me show my appreciation by helping you get what you want.
- This entire office depends on your accuracy, so let's set up a check system so we learn from this mistake.
- Your track record is excellent, but there is one area for improvement that takes time to master. I'm putting you with Michael until you're proficient. Most of us have had to learn this in this way.

"

Without continual growth
and progress, such words as
improvement, achievement, and
success have no meaning.

—Benjamin Franklin

"

Below is my scale of emotional well-being; it provides me with a visual cue to how I am feeling. It also gives me insight into others when they are communicating with me. I suggest making your own list or personalizing my list and having a good mental visual connection to your emotional scale. Self-awareness, striving for improvement, and mindfulness of how you feel in the present moment is a powerful tool that allows you to grow as a person.

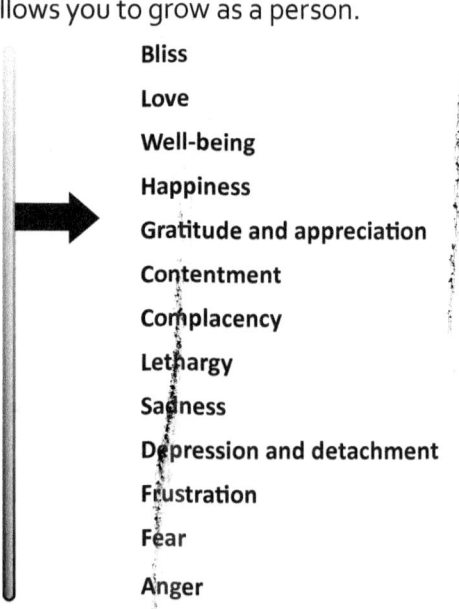

Bliss

Love

Well-being

Happiness

Gratitude and appreciation

Contentment

Complacency

Lethargy

Sadness

Depression and detachment

Frustration

Fear

Anger

PERSPECTIVES ON CHANGING YOUR PERSPECTIVE

Each mind is unique, much in the same way that fingerprints differ from person to person. Male to female, brother to brother, sister or sister, our minds are complex and vary widely according to genetic and environmental influences. What is true for one person is not true for another, even within the same family. Our diversity is what makes us autonomous and so profoundly successful as a species.

When you look at the illustrations below, think about how they relate to your personal perspective.

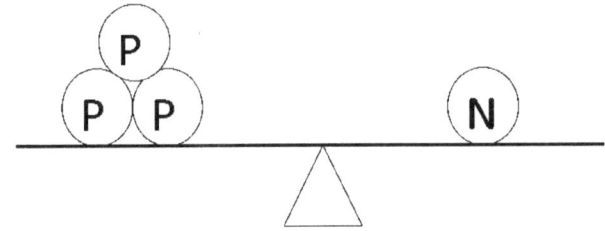

In my personal perspective, the negative attributes, or negative weight, of an average negative topic is about 3 to 1, as shown above compared to positive. In other words if you were to weigh positive and negative topics based on their emotional impact, the above illustration would be accurate for me. (For the purposes of the illustration, the positive items have little to no weight.)

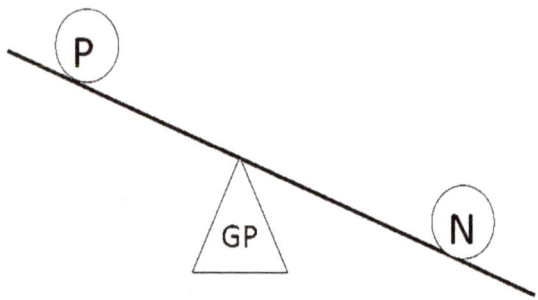

Your general perspective is a pivot point, or GP in the illustration above. Since negative outweighs positive, shifting your GP creates improved balance and resiliency when negative circumstances or issues occur. If you are experiencing even a single negative issue, it upsets your personal balance and makes it more difficult to deal with, even with a positive influence present.

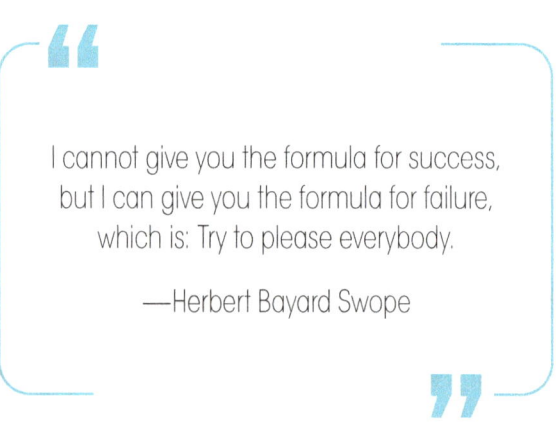

I cannot give you the formula for success, but I can give you the formula for failure, which is: Try to please everybody.

—Herbert Bayard Swope

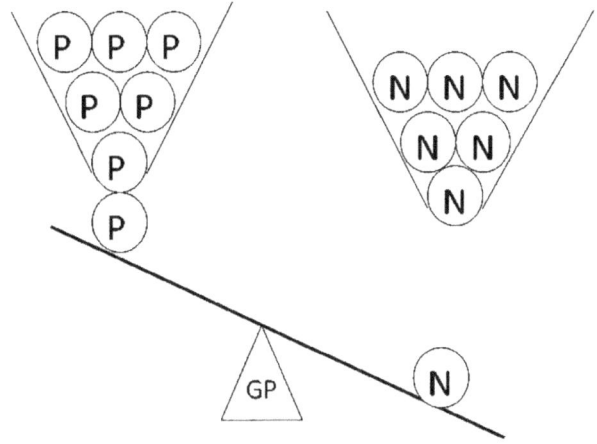

One of the main issues with always focusing on the negative or always having a negative topic on your mind is that you block the incoming positive emotions and circumstances. This is a self-inhibiting, self-perpetuating mental cycle that traps some people for an entire lifetime. We all have met people caught in this cycle; no matter how hard they try, they cannot ignore an opportunity to wallow in the negativity that comes their way every day. Chances are, if something positive did come their way, they would be suspicious and look for the underlying negativity.

We all need to stay focused on the positive aspects of our lives and to be self-aware enough to know when a change of focus is needed. When you are out of balance, you need to shift your general perspective (GP).

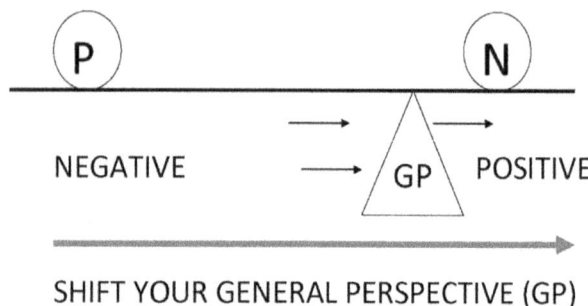

SHIFT YOUR GENERAL PERSPECTIVE (GP)

When you are in balance, negative topics and issues have very little impact and do not upset your sense of well-being. The change process involves creating a sense of gratitude and pointing out all the things to be grateful for each day. This shifts your general perspective in a positive direction and prevents any tipping points. In a sense, you protect yourself from the negativity of others and don't buy into negative cycles.

When you are balanced to the positive, you learn to love life and place yourself in an open, receptive state. You start to reinforce each part of your current reality that you love, which perpetuates positive movement away from negative circumstances, people, and environments. This mind-over-matter state shifts you into a mental state of getting exactly what you want. And what could be better than that?

Shifting perspective on a broader spectrum than the green lights example given earlier takes time and dedication to mindfulness or self-awareness. Most of us are well aware of areas in our lives that are not working as well as what we would like. Shifting our focus or general perspective from negative to positive begins with the desire to create a change, whether it has a small or large impact on your current reality. Removing all blame of others and yourself and focusing on the desired result, puts you in a mind-set or mind-over- matter state that facilitates the desired change.

It may be necessary to repeat this process many times to shift your GP into the balanced state, as seen in the previous illustration. But if it is truly what you desire, then building the perspective for the desired changes is a labor of love that perpetuates you the success you want.

Here are ten mind-over-matter steps to success:

1. Decide what you would like to change.
2. Discover what it is that you truly want as an end result.
3. Break down the end result into details until you can identify with the positive emotion that the change will bring.
4. Build a list of known processes and actions needed to make this happen.
5. List all positive aspects of the change and change process, and revise and review as often as possible.
6. Add as much positive emotion and good thoughts about the desired changes as possible.

7. Research the end result, talk to others that have made the change, and be willing to commit fully to the process.

8. The more energy you put into the process, the sooner the change will happen.

9. Stay balanced with rest, diet, and exercise. You are less likely to succeed if you are out there on the ragged edge.

10. Be true to yourself. If you know in your heart that this is what you want, then it is right. Trust your inner guidance and instincts and be willing to modify your current perspective on what will be great for you.

"

Insanity is doing the same
thing, over and over again, but
expecting different results.

—Narcotics Anonymous

"

HOW POSITIVE ARE YOU REALLY?

On a scale of 1 to 10, how often do you show these emotions? 10 is every day; 7 is often; 5 is sometimes; 3 is rarely; and 0 is never.

Rate each question and total your score independently for parts 1 and 2.

Remember, you have to really think about your answers and be as honest as possible to get an accurate result on your view of how you perceive you.

Interestingly, you may want a loved one or relative to complete the quiz for you to get an outsider's perspective.

Part 1

1. Fun loving, spontaneous playfulness
2. Amazed, awed, full of wonder
3. Appreciative, grateful
4. Hopeful, encouraged, optimistic
5. Easily moved, uplifted, inspired
6. Laughs a lot, even to tears
7. Loves, expressed deep affection

8. Proud, uplifted
9. Sublime, at peace, complete
10. Praises others with emotion

Part 2

11. Nervous, stressed
12. Irritated, annoyed
13. Humiliated, ashamed
14. Critical of people (comments or thoughts with emotion)
15. Critical of situations
16. Repulsed, disgusted
17. Guilty, remorseful
18. Hateful, distrusting
19. Unhappy, sad, depressed
20. Vocalizes anger toward self or others

Assessing your score

Add up your score for parts 1 and 2 separately, so you will have a positive and a negative score.

Using this scale, it is easy to see which way you are leaning and what areas need work to shift your focus more to the positive side.

A balanced score is two-thirds positive and one-third negative. The more positive and less negative the better.

Assessing your score in part 1

75 to 100

You may be a monk! You likely spend much of your day in a mindfulness state with much success and gratitude. If you have scored in this range, you are in the top 5 percent of all the people in North America, or your responses are wishful thinking. Either way, it is something that we all should aspire to. Getting here often takes a lifetime of dedication to filtering out the things in our environment that we feel are not a priority in our lives. When you get into this level of thinking, life is inspirational, and each day is a blessing filled with excitement and awe.

50 to 75

This is a great score! When you can exceed 50 percent, you are in the top 20 percent of North Americans. This is what most people are capable of, given the environment most are subjected to each day. It takes consistent awareness of yourself and attention to your mind to get to this level. I congratulate you!

I know that you have a positive influence on everyone around you, and this greatly adds quality of life to those in your circles and will influences others for generations.

0 to 50

Congratulations! You are in with the rest of us. If you have score 50 or below, you have work to do to clean up the negative thoughts that hold you back. Work daily, little by little, as you clean up your thinking. By being attentive to desired results, you will begin to see only what pleases you. As you tip the balance toward a positive state of mind, joy, harmony, and success will flow into your life through the positive doors you open.

Assessing your score in part 2

The very best you could score in part 2 is zero; less is more when it comes to negative thoughts and reactions to negative things in your environment. As you change your focus toward the positive, your negative score can and will drop quickly and dramatically. As you shift your attention to what you like and what you really like, you won't notice the negative aspects of your world that made you unhappy. Isn't it absolutely wonderful that you now know you have absolute control over your happiness and success?

0 to 25

Nice job. This is the optimum zone, which indicates limited to no negativity. It is actually not difficult to achieve a score in this zone with mindfulness, or mind-over-matter thinking, being in the moment, and not reacting without thought to your environment.

25 to 50

Well, you guessed it. There is room for improvement. The majority of the population will likely score in this zone. Targeting a personal goal of less than 20 is attainable for most people.

50 and up

If you scored above 50, you really have work to do. You likely feel you are stuck in a negative environment, so making incremental changes can ease the transition into being more positive. Identifying patterns of negativity and identifying what you really want in life can be the first steps to a fresh start.

The more you know who you
are and what you want, the
less you let things upset you.

—Stephanie Perkins

SHIFTING YOUR MIND UP AND OUT OF A NEGATIVE CYCLE

There are long-term and short-term tools and perspectives for shifting out of a negative thinking cycle. Let me start by saying that any negative thoughts only hurt you, or at least inhibit you from getting what you want. As you consistently voice or think negative thoughts about someone or something, you take away positive energy or thoughts regarding positive movement forward for yourself.

For the short term, creating a list of the positive aspects of any self-inhibiting subject will slowly cause a shift in what you believe to be true about that subject. The trick is to build your list and add positive emotion as you reread and reinforce the list in your mind. Read the list each time negative feelings are felt.

After you have completed this process a few times, you will be able to start to shift into mind-over-matter thinking without lists and recognize problems long before they start. This is the long-term work. This long-term work has changed my life into a more joyful journey. Many forward-thinking people recognize that life is about just that—the journey. And the big things that make the trip more enjoyable start from the inside.

In the next section are some examples of the *positive aspects process*. When you catch yourself saying you *hate* or cannot stand something, this is a cue to yourself that action is needed to change this thought pattern.

> "
>
> Too many of us are not
> living our dreams because
> we are living our fears.
>
> —Les Brown
>
> "

THE POSITIVE ASPECTS PROCESS

Changing your perspective is straight-forward; you must be true to yourself about the emotions that anchor your beliefs in your mind about a topic. You cannot make any headway toward positive change if you believe in the negative aspects of that topic. Below are some examples of changing your negative views about goals and money.

To change your thoughts, you need to make a list of all the good things or positive aspects of a given topic, while ignoring your current feelings and beliefs. Avoid direct opposites of what you currently believe to be true; find positive aspects that make sense to you; and revisit your list often as you feel negative feelings. This process may seem difficult at first, but it truly works well if you honestly desire positive change.

Existing Negative Thoughts	New Positive Thoughts
I cannot afford a new vehicle.	They have low-interest financing. I can budget my finances better. A new vehicle seems to last longer. Buying a slightly used car is possible. I will save a lot of repair costs on my old car. I love all the new technology. The fuel economy is excellent. I love the new car smell. The year-end models are reduced.
Money is hard to come by.	I deserve money as much as the next person. I have many options to bring in more money. I feel better when I have saved some money. It comes and goes; it's just life. I always have enough.
I don't have the skill to win.	I have yet to reach the top of my game. I to win. will get the skills I need to excel. With the right coaching, I can push my boundaries. I can do anything I want bad enough. I can see, smell, and taste the victory!
The economy is holding me back.	The economy is always changing. I can always move or find extra income. I'm going to watch the news less. I can spend less; I have what I need. They really need a good news channel.

By not taking the emotional hit, you protect your subconscious from logging into the emotion, which in turn prevents you from escalating the feelings and adding mental blocks to positive movement forward regarding the topic of concern. When you recognize the negative issues before they compound, you are on the right track to positive change.

Positive aspects about people

I hate my boss; he holds me back.	His character issues don't affect me. His agenda will not dampen my spirit. I will rise above him soon. I can learn a lot here. Everyone else is so great. I can see beyond him easily. He is rarely there. His negativity bounces off. He has good qualities. There are so many other good reasons to stay.
I hate those people.	They really don't know better. Things will change soon. All things change; so will they. I have other options. I don't see them often. I enjoy working with their competition. I hardly notice them anymore. That woman is nice; she tries hard. They are doing their best. They have a nice facility.

When you judge another, you do not define them, you define yourself.

—Wayne Dyer

Positive aspects worksheet

Take your pet peeves and work out the positive aspects of those people or situations. Try for a minimum of ten, but more is better. Think about your list. Read it for a few days, and try to add more positive aspects. You will find that this process lifts a weight off your shoulders; you will feel lighter because you are not carrying around burdens of negativity.

Sample Worksheet

I really dislike my job

It does give me some new skills
It is just a stepping stone to something better
I have met a lot of new friends there
I do get weekends off
I really enjoy my breaks
My co workers make me laugh
It's not too far from my home
It has a great restaurant and coffee shop near by
The pay is not great but covers my bills easily
The staff had an amazing Christmas party last year
I like it when I get to change work stations
I don't have worry about layoffs
It's a nice warm place to work in the winter

An important part of this mind-over-matter exercise is that you not ever list anything that *you do not believe is true as you see it today.* You cannot instantly change your mind about what you believe about a given topic.

This process most often can tip the balance in the perception of what you generally believe to be true. When you make the mental shift, it is amazing how this process can be transformational. Apply it over all the negative aspects of your life, and begin to reap the many rewards of a positive mind-set.

"

Conflict cannot survive
without your participation.

—Wayne Dyer

"

A POSITIVE ASPECTS TRANSITION STORY

Here is a rather amazing story about how a positive perspective can change the direction of your life.

In my thirties, I was a busy building contractor. As a journeyman carpenter and employer, I wore many hats. Bidding work, running jobs, organizing materials, working with subcontractors such as electricians or plumbers, dealing with people, ensuring job quality, timelines, and budgets left me little time to reflect on my personal perspectives. I often found myself exhausted, lying awake at night going over the day's activities and projecting events in my mind of the upcoming day.

As I pushed everyone around me toward their best performance and workmanship, I often found myself in conflict with people and situations beyond my control. It seemed to me that fewer people on staff and unrestricted timelines took away the pressure of the daily need to produce perceived perfection of the end product.

It became apparent to me that when these factors were compressed together, something had to give, and any resolution would cost money on the project. Some projects were music to my ears; like a well-choreographed recital, the synergy flowed. Other projects with added obstacles, such as restricted timelines, weather, site conditions, or access, became taxing and spawned negativity. It seemed that even with the best possible effort, the project was going to run off the rails and budget.

I started to notice a pattern that developed from experience; I began to recognize that many different types of projects were not worth pursuing.

As I broke down the business into its fundamental qualities and defined the uplifting aspects of the business that the staff and I enjoyed most, it was much more enjoyable and easier to see the future from a positive perspective. As I identified the unwanted aspects and the desired aspects of projects, locations, and site conditions, it became apparent what kind of projects we preferred to be involved with.

Some projects are taxing on manpower, resources, and logistics. A consensus with the staff and a willingness to take less risk with less pay enabled our company to operate smoothly. Looking back at the sequence of events at that time, removing the pressure to make money and grow the business at any cost removed the stress and allowed us to enjoy what we were good at and allowed us to come home at night to our families.

All too often people lose sight of what's important. Perpetuating a business just because opportunity presents itself is a good idea only if balance can be maintained. Ultimately everyone should maintain a clear picture of what is wanted. Success, clarity, a strong family union, joy, and harmony become the focus instead of someone else's unrealistic deadlines. When you define success for you, look deeply into what is important to you. This will help you sustain long-term happiness and prosperity.

> Identifying what is ultimately important to you with clarity and emotion trumps all other cards in the deck.

WE LIVE BETTER
THAN KINGS

We are highly successful as an evolved species. Compare us to any other mammal on the planet. If you were anything other than a human, you would not be enjoying the shelter, food, communication, health care, and transportation of our highly evolved, technological society.

It is said the over 95 percent of the world's best scientists are alive today. The speed of human evolution is apparent all around us; every day there are advancements on every scientific frontier.

You were born into this highly evolved society, into a generation that would build on all of the accomplishments and technology of all the previous generations combined.

We all now live better than any king throughout history. The availability, quantity, quality, and selection of food rival that of any king. Our homes, with their modern conveniences and comforts, far exceed that of any king. Take away power, indoor plumbing, central heating, and entertainment systems, and see how well you are doing, regardless of how many staff and rooms you have. Transportation is also light-years beyond anything even just one hundred years ago.

When you take stock, you begin to appreciate who and where we are. As we look about the big picture, we see we are super successful as a group or species, and all we have to do to feel blessed by the abundance and success is to stop to appreciate it. You can stand on the threshold of tomorrow and look at the awe and wonderment of everything in this big, bright, beautiful world or not; it's up to you. Really, your life perspective is simply mind over matter.

"

The secret of living a life of
excellence is merely a matter of
thinking thoughts of excellence.
Really, it's a matter of programming
our minds with the kind of
information that will set us free.

—Charles R. Swindoll

"

Be mindful when communicating with others

Consider that your personal perspective of yourself may not always be shared by others, in that your perception is unique to you and is a self-imposed condition that is a result of your mental conditioning to this point in your life. You most likely cannot see this, but you sense it in your interactions with others.

Further, consider that you have preloaded, preconditioned mental reaction states or templates for each of thousands of scenarios when you react to events or have a verbal exchange with anyone. To get a sense of this, picture yourself talking with different types of people. You talk much differently to family members than you would to a famous person. If you were that famous person, how would you react to a group of fans or a group of well-wishing people?

The question here is, can you see what the other person or group sees in you? Consider that if you often find yourself in a defensive exchange, you are not likely in sync with the person or party you are having the exchange with.

Picture yourself or imagine yourself interacting with someone you just met. How you react to this individual is highly dependent on many preconditioned factors:

- appearance
- gender
- age
- occupation
- familiarity
- environment
- emotional preconditions

If the person you are speaking with is behind a wall or curtain, and you do not have any visual or audio information, you likely will communicate very differently to this person, because you will not have the visual cues to prejudge this person and apply one of your preconditioned responses. You would struggle to discern if it is a man or woman, adult or child, as you likely have different degrees of comfort and exchange differently with each group.

Our personal perceptions and personal conditioning play a much larger role in our communication with others than most people realize. Mindfulness of yourself and your preconceived patterns of thought is one way to recognize that you can grow as a person and be much more successful if you step back and read yourself and others. Defensive people and people who have blocked out positive emotion have walled themselves into a cell where very little growth is possible. For many, this can be a life sentence.

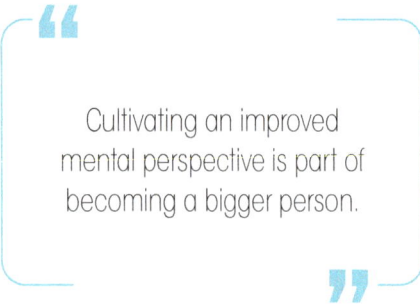

> Cultivating an improved mental perspective is part of becoming a bigger person.

Be present in the moment

Mindfulness of your own character and reactions is part of getting into the moment and not reacting with conditioned, mindless responses.

Training yourself to be present in the moment has many advantages. It allows you to grow as a person, improves your perception of self, and allows you to better understand what other people see in you. It improves your sense of well-being, improves confidence, and inspires others to positive change.

Here are some interaction traits to improve by being mindful of what you're saying in the moment:

- talking down to others, such as children or minorities
- being defensive or guarded and using deflective dialogue
- having reactive, knee-jerk responses
- mocking and participating in abrasive dialogue
- being confrontational or offensive
- using sarcasm

Each of these responses is a conditioned reaction that require your attention if you are to have improved mind-over-matter thinking. Easing your preconditioned feelings will have a dramatic effect on people around you.

Our senses allow us to feel others emotions within seconds of communicating. We instinctively know exactly how the individual is feeling, and we react immediately with one of our preconditioned responses.

It is possible to gauge your emotional preconditioned responses. When you work at removing negative emotion from your responses, so that *you do not feel or allow in the emotion from another, it* enables *you to maintain control in the moment* and not build a highly volatile, reactive scenario. Ridged emotional defense mechanisms can and will override the mind, as one emotional response perpetuates and elevates responses from the other person.

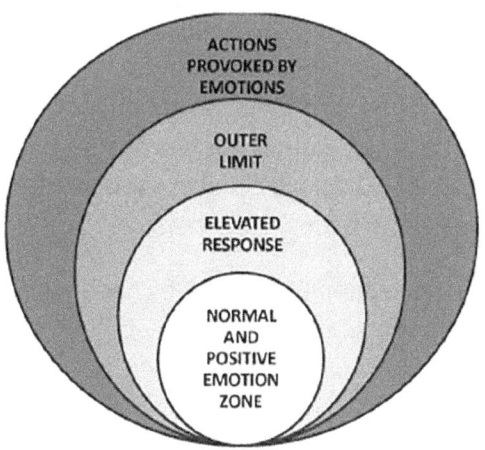

Interactions with family members can be the most challenging due to years of conditioning. Observing yourself in the interaction moment and recognizing moments of tension and displeasure allows you to regulate your emotional responses. Without proper preparation, you will likely get swept up in the negativity of others.

Learning to accept people for who they are and allowing them to be limited in their own thinking allows you to step away from the emotional trap of engaging in redundant condescending dialogue. Allowing others to come to terms with their own reality and with life lessons can help them recognize what they do not want.

It is possible to disarm provoking dialogue by offering sentiments of love, respect, and value. Point out that you desire harmony and do not make emotionally provoking comments to the people you care most about. Inspiring others with uplifting examples and positive reinforcement removes tension. And of course the most uplifting example uses action, not words. As a parent or mentor, you cannot teach unless you teach by example, if you do not believe in the words you are saying, you cannot convince others.

Your personal example of positive change, combined with encouragement, can do much more than a lifetime of scolding or criticism.

"

True freedom is attained by
releasing yourself from your mental
connection to the negativity
of others and by maintaining
a clear perspective of self.

"

WHAT ARE YOU
REALLY SAYING?

Learn to talk the talk and walk the walk in a confident way, not being funny, goofy, or arrogant. As you work on self-talk, look at others' posture and body language. What are they saying? When it comes down to it, you might be inhibiting your communication with important people if you don't come across as reputable or believable. Do you remember the old saying "Your appearance speaks so loudly, I can't hear what you're saying." In today's business climate, a large part of your success is communication. There are three main parts to effective communication.

- appearance
- body language
- clarity of speech

*Appearance i*s an important issue, to be sure, because if you dress for success, it shows; but the opposite is also true. Today there is more tolerance for fashion statements; the key is to dress in a way that makes you feel good and also portrays a message to others that makes you look credible. Obviously, if either of these is not in place, it takes away from the mental and physical aspects of the intended goal when communicating with others.

Body language can work for you or against you. In my experience, this can be one of the most difficult items to change or improve. This is because it is habitual; your current body language was formed over a lifetime of conditioning, and your future body language must be formed into a new habit. It takes thirty days to form a new permanent habit.

Watch people you admire and mirror their body language. Take notes and practice. Good books on this subject are also available. Body language is a real confidence booster when used properly. As you perfect your communications with successful people, you feel great, and doors open up for you.

Clarity of speech is knowing what you want and conveying that message in an effective manner. When you do your "due diligence," when you know everything there is to know on a subject, and when you know exactly what you want from each meeting or conversation, then you are poised to get what you want. Listen to good communicators; learn to identify who they are and who resonates with you. Practice great communication with your friends and business associates, and above all be prepared and confident going into any meeting.

If you truly desire change,
you must be willing to think
and act differently.

GET YOUR HEAD
IN THE GAME

A big part of your personal success is self-discipline. It can be the most challenging aspect to maintain over the long term, but the benefits can change your mood and stamina. To operate at peak capacity, you have to have energy and feel good. Rest, diet, and exercise are more difficult to maintain as you get older, and if you have let yourself go for a long time, the road back can be quite long. If that is the case, additional help and motivation from others may be required. The process is itself a life-changing experience. When you feel great, your mind is sharp and you radiate vitality to others. You also perpetuate your personal success.

Habitual lifestyle changes are not easy at first; it takes thirty days of repetitive actions to form a permanent change.

Rest is highly underrated. As you age, rest becomes more and more important. Some people seem happy to run on stimulants all day every day, and I guess as I look back to my twenties, I wasn't much different. Coffee, Red Bull, or pounding back extra-large Slurpees from 7-Eleven is obviously not sustainable even on a daily basis, as it leads to an energy crash and can have long-term effects on your health. Whenever possible, remove stress and reset your mind by closing your eyes for a few moments. It may be possible slip out to your vehicle during lunch breaks for a few minutes of a meditative type of rest. This action is in harmony with your body and mind, which has not evolved to put out endlessly day after day.

Another important part of getting your head in the game is diet. Removing processed foods and adding a vitamin supplement regime have greatly improved my stamina and sense of well-being. If you want to feel good, you have to make lifestyle choices that do exactly that: make you feel great.

I suggest doing research and then setting absolute minimums for exercise. There are many great books on sustaining a healthy, active lifestyle. One piece of advice I found very useful is the forty-minute rule. The book *You: The Owner's Manual* by Dr. Michael F. Roizen and Dr. Mehmet Oz states that the human body requires a minimum of forty minutes of exercise three times per week at the heart rate for your age and weight category. I love this open-ended cardio workout, as it can apply to any indoor or outdoor activity as long as it achieves the minimum goal.

When it comes down to your mind and body, taking care of your body really is everything to you, and as you age, you have to *move it or lose it*.

> ➢ Make a point of resting your mind and body by closing your eyes for five to fifteen minutes

at least twice during the day, possibly at lunch break and upon arriving home. You will be amazed how quickly your body adapts and responds with natural energy.

➢ Change your diet to add more essential fatty acids, such as fish, nuts, avocados, and fresh fruit.

➢ Research vitamins and other supplements that will naturally support your mind and body.

➢ Meet your minimum exercise quota of forty minutes of sustained cardio three times every week for your age and weight.

(Always consult with your doctor before starting an exercise program.)

"

Do not go where the path may
lead, go instead where there
is no path and leave a trail.

—Ralph Waldo Emerson

"

THE RIGHT MENTAL TOOLS ARE
THE SEEDS FOR CHANGE

Having a larger, clear goal process is like planning and constructing a beautiful new home.

As part of the planning process and well before any action is taken, you must envision your desired outcome with as much clarity and focus as possible. This step must come first. Do your research; get to know the exact look and feel of your end result. Obtaining books on the subject helps give you insight into what you really like. Compile as much information as possible as you gain clarity and emotional attachments to the features that resonate with your desires.

Once information is collected, sum up the end result and connect with it as best you can. See it in your mind as completed. Walk through the home in your mind, drinking in the features, comfort, benefits, and view. Project yourself into the future, enjoying the good feeling of living in the home.

It does not matter if this project is ten months or ten years into your future; the goal here is clarity. If you know exactly what you want, you will naturally gravitate toward the how and the when, unless you change your focus. When you take one step closer to your dream, such as purchasing the property on which your dream home will be built or securing financing, your conviction that it is inevitable that the dreams will coalesce into reality and will become rock solid in your mind.

In this example, there thousands of action items that must be followed to ensure that the project goes as planned. When you have completed your mental preparation, it creates flow and synergy, because you know exactly what you want, down to the last detail.

A similar, more basic example is an Indy NASCAR driver who desires victory. Often the positive thinking of driver is formed through a lifelong desire; that desire slowly manifests into an actual career. When the driver was a child, the desire was a make-believe dream. That dream grew with time, and the more the boy or girl built emotional attachment to the dream and stayed with it, the more circumstances came to fruition.

As the goal focus changed to winning, the driver's emotional attachment to the goal was the primary component to bring about the change. Many negative elements could have derailed the driver's success, such as lack of confidence or fear of any number of obstacles or events. This is when extra mental preparation in the process was needed to shift the focus to the intended outcome and away from any negative influences.

The thing always happens
that you really believe in;
***and the belief in a
thing*** makes it happen.

—Frank Lloyd Wright

THE MENTAL CONNECTION: VISUALIZATION

Can you see it? Your victory day, your pinnacle achievement—what does it look like? Who is there? Is it an Olympic podium moment or the opening day of your very own business? No matter what your goal, it has a defining moment that you can tune into, build in detail, and build into the emotional rush and elation of your defining moment.

Really tune into your moment and write down as many details of your dream as possible. Once you have it down, read it and embellish it, adding more details every time you deeply connect. Here are some questions and guidelines to assist you in building a clear, deep connection with your goal.

> ➢ Where does your defining moment take place?
> ➢ Describe the environment in as much detail as possible.
> ➢ Who is there to share this moment?
> ➢ Is it day or night?
> ➢ What are the tangible items that make this time special?
> ➢ What is the weather like?
> ➢ What sounds are present?

- ➤ Are there smells associated with this moment?
- ➤ Describe your feelings.
- ➤ Describe the feelings of others present.
- ➤ What further details can you add?

> If you change the way you look at things, the things you look at change.
>
> —Wayne Dyer

HOW DO YOU REALLY GET TUNED IN, TAPPED IN, AND TURNED ON?

Become *one* with the process and the goal!

The Olympic champion has taken the event, broken the process down, and mentally merged with the process. Every detail, every move, every piece of equipment is fine-tuned over and over until there is symmetry between the body and mind. This takes the goal to the ultimate level; the mind is so fine-tuned with the action that specific thoughts are rarely needed, because the mind and body are the process.

This is the *eye of the tiger*—the ultimate cutting edge of human conditioning and perfection. When all of this comes together, it is like poetry in motion. Everything is as it should be and will be, because it can be nothing else. It is *perfection*.

Now, how do we apply this to our everyday goals?

1. Commit wholeheartedly to the process and end result.
2. Define and redefine the goal and process until it is perfect.
3. Rework the mental attachment into an obsession.

4. See, smell, and taste the full excitement of the victory moment.
5. Commit time and emotions to achieve daily progress.
6. *Stay the course:* burn the goal into your mind until you dream of nothing else.

I suggest you *do not* start your plan unless you make a personal commitment to apply yourself with 150 percent honesty and intent to create permanent lifestyle changes. Be clear about what you are going to do and when it is going to take place. Many people are looking for "the competitive edge." Some will skim this book to glean bits of information to apply to their daily ambitions. But remember that it took a lifetime of conditioning to get you to where you are today, and changes take time. Again, it takes thirty days to form a habit, good or bad. Use your calendar to track your progress on thirty-day benchmarks for achieving your goals.

This is not a quick fix, but a highly doable journey. I urge you to make a wholehearted commitment to your goal, if you truly desire change.

Example of plans to become a helicopter pilot

Goals for week 1

- ✓ Collect information on employment opportunities.
- ✓ List all potential employers, national and international.

✓ List questions for employers.
✓ List all training facilities.

Week 2

✓ List questions for active pilots.
✓ Talk to as many active pilots as possible (drop into airfields).
✓ Talk to employers regarding appointments.

Week 3

✓ Talk to training facilities.
✓ List questions regarding courses, costs, availability, success rates, duration.
✓ Find our which advanced training courses will be needed in the future.
✓ Find out the long-term training required for future endorsements in the field.

Week 4

✓ Set interim training date, allowing time for saving money.
✓ Look at other course options for the interim.
✓ Find others with similar goals, potential study partners.
✓ Look into associations of clubs for pilots and online forums.

Questions for existing helicopter employers

- Is their work seasonal?
- When do they typically hire?

- What kind of people or credentials are in demand?
- Are there any openings presently?
- Is the work part-time or full-time?
- What are the yearly earnings for first-year pilots and seasoned professionals?
- Is one training facility better recognized than others?
- What are the pitfalls for pilots in this industry?

Week 5

- ✓ Create a schedule to learn more about how to be successful in the industry.
- ✓ Target a course end date.
- ✓ Look at ground school for a fixed-wing license.
- ✓ Get available course material for early study.

In this example, there are a lot of variables and unknowns, but the goal is clear, and there is a willingness to do whatever it takes and to set the steps into an attainable, traceable timeline. Maintaining a clear end point in this case is more challenging, but building excitement by keeping the goal in the forefront of your mind daily and making daily progress keeps the goal fresh and on track to the end point.

BUILDING A POSITIVE MIND-SET

Building a more general positive perspective is a matter of mental conditioning and recognizing areas for improvement. In some difficult negative environments, it may be necessary to move yourself away from the toxic influences of others.

Moving to joy or positivity starts with recognizing how you feel at any moment and making course corrections or mood alterations a little bit at a time. Introducing new words into your vocabulary is a nice easy way to make the shift gradually.

Keep in mind that trying to make a large shift or quantum leap forward can leave you with a sense of despair or unease. Your mind has a very well-entrenched comfort zone, and not exceeding your personal boundaries or beliefs is necessary for a successful transition.

Here is a short list of my favorite positive statements, which I use in self-talk to support a positive mind-set. I suggest introducing these or similar words as often as possible, in a conscience effort to make a shift into a more joyful perspective.

It's all good
It was my pleasure
Makes my day
I love...
The funniest thing
The most amazing
It's going to be great
The most incredible
It was to die for
I'm so lucky/ blessed
I was blown away
I can't believe it

absolutely
amazing
beautiful
excellent
exciting
fun
funny
handsome
happy
healthy
impressive
joy
laugh
lucky
masterful
meaningful
motivating
moving
nice
optimistic
paradise
perfect
phenomenal
pleasurable

plentiful
pleasant
positive
powerful
pretty
protected
proud
remarkable
resounding
rewarding
smile
stunning
success
super
terrific
thrilling
unreal
vibrant
victorious
wonderful
wondrous
wow
yes
unbelievable

"

Identify your problems but give your
power and energy to solutions.

—Tony Robbins

"

REPROGRAMMING YOUR MIND
WITH POSITIVITY

I have personally used this method to cause a large shift in the way I feel in general from day to day. It has had a huge effect on my children and spouse. Funny thing is that since this shift happened, it feels as if things have always been this way.

Also, the shift was gradual enough that other family members did not recognize or remember the shift happening. It seemed to take some time for the trickledown effect, but it finally took root into a more positive household. In the beginning I was criticized because my behavior was not perceived as normal. Now it seems they correct me if I default out of what they perceive as normal for me.

If you are feeling worn down by less-than-thankful individuals or stress from your environment and desire a significant change, try changing your perspective from the inside out. As you make the shift to think and act differently, your environment follows suit.

I love this quote from Bashar: "Life is a mirror. What you put out is what you get back."

Here are few exercises to get you started.

❖ Take each starter phrase and add as many words as you can to form a sentence. Feel free to add your words and phrases to personalize the list. Note how you feel after this one simple task of focusing on mental positive thoughts.

❖ Find four or five words on your list, and make a point to use these words as many times as possible for an entire day.

Take note of any differences in your day, and continue this process until the process becomes second nature, which will take at least thirty days.

Start your day with uplifting words or a favorite quote, and set out each morning looking for all the positive aspects of your life that can give you a beautiful, uplifted feeling.

When you squeeze an orange,
orange juice comes out—
because that's what's inside.
When you are squeezed, what
comes out is what is inside.

—Wayne Dyer

COMPLIMENTS:
THE GOLDEN GIFT THAT GIVES BACK

M ind-over-matter thinking is altering your perception and the perception of others in a positive manner. Your success partly depends on how well you get along with people. If you don't take the time to notice and positively interact with others, chances are they may be overlooking you as well. When you know the right thoughts and course of action, you empower yourself and prosper.

Have you ever taken notice of the power of a *genuine* compliment? It has the instant effect of uplifting the recipient and often includes a good feeling for the provider as well. Genuine compliments or your personal, kind approval makes the recipients feel good about themselves, boosting their confidence and improving their outlook. In most cases, the warmed recipient garners good feelings that improve the relationship with the compliment provider.

To give compliments, you have to like yourself and genuinely like other people. If you cannot give a genuine compliment, you need to seek out help in these areas. Often a good friend can help bring you out of your current comfort zone.

Here are some examples of genuine compliments:
Family

I really appreciate it when you...
I noticed you have really given this effort.
That was very kind of you.
You really did awesome.
I love you for your thoughtfulness.
That was perfect timing.

Coworkers

I love what you're wearing (to women).
Your professional appearance has not gone unnoticed (to men).
I am impressed with your actions.
You really care about this; I like that.
Your work station is an example to others.
You have come a long way.
What a great question!

Athletes

You are incredible.
The team is showing true progress today.
I love your determination.
It's really great to have you as a teammate.
Your help has made all the difference.
Thanks to you, we have this.

This powerful tool is not to be overlooked. Look for opportunities to compliment others daily. Start with a low number, such as two compliments, and push that number to six. Be careful not to compliment any one person more than twice a day, because others may think something is up. Continue this process for at least thirty days. You will be amazed at the change in your relationships with everyone.

"

I can live for two months
on a good compliment.

—Mark Twain

"

LONG-TERM GRATITUDE IS A MIND-OVER-MATTER TRANSFORMATIVE POWER TOOL

Success in life or as a person is subjective; in other words, what is defined as success for one person is not necessarily success for the next person. If you are happy and have the experiences and material things that your heart desires, you are successful.

For some people, an ultimate achievement of some sort is their definition of success. Most of us do not have to scale Everest or K2 to have a sense of accomplishment or self-worth. If success can be defined as true happiness, finding your own person level of contentment or peace of mind is a critical component to your success as a person. In the end, it is you aligning with you. Developing an attitude of gratitude will make a difference in your perspective and is an attractive quality that can perpetuate success in other areas of your life. Expanding your perception of success will bring more appreciation into your life and make you feel more successful in your current situation. As you align with good feelings, it perpetuates positive change and creates momentum in that direction.

Synonyms of gratitude include *thankfulness*, *appreciation*, and *gratefulness*.

Gratitude can take on several forms, both short term and long term. In the short term, gratitude is reciprocity, being thankful for someone's action, such as an unexpected gift or act or generosity. In the long-term, it really is the development of a general attitude of gratefulness for your life. Like most mind-over-matter disciplines, it takes a clear focus toward the intended result and effort over time to reorient your current pattern of thinking.

Benefits of long-term gratitude

Part of being successful in the outer environment is having it together in your mind—your inner environment. Attitudes of confidence and self-worth are qualities of great leaders and employees. People invest in sharp, vibrant, enthusiastic individuals.

> *Gratitude detaches you from stress in your environment.*
> When you start to appreciate your life and you are thankful for all the good things in it, you no longer stress about or take notice of the things you don't care for.

> *It reduces self-imposed stress.*
> You are less self-critical, and you accept your environment as a temporary, changing condition that you will evolve from.

> *It improves your health.*

A state of gratitude has been known to lower blood pressure and promoted longevity, as noted in the lives of monks.

It improves quality of life.
When you approach life from a "have" instead of a "have not" perspective due to gratitude, you naturally feel better about your abundance.

It changes your relationships with people.
People recognize positivity, and most people find it to be an attractive quality.

It improves your self-esteem.
When people have great things to say about you and your attitude, it perpetuates more of the same.

It improves your sense of well-being.
Gratitude is thankfulness. When you are grateful for today, you look forward to tomorrow, grounding your sense of well-being.

Gratitude opens you up to more positive experiences.
When you perpetuate a state of gratitude, you are open and receptive to more of the same, which draws you into similar future experiences.

"

Seek pleasure everywhere, and it
will be your gift just for looking.

"

HOW DO YOU GET
THERE FROM HERE?

I magine yourself experiencing the benefits mentioned on the last few pages. Take a moment and visually connect with each of the listed items. Can you more deeply connect with one or more on the list? If you can, this is your best starting point. When you identify with a feeling or emotion, you are actually making a connection in your mind that you can build on.

Identify with these items throughout your day and list things that happened that caused a feeling of *thankfulness, appreciation, and gratefulness.* Another excellent way to promote feelings of thankfulness, appreciation, and gratitude is to look for opportunities to offer acts of kindness. I have had a long-standing personal motto: "Never turn down an opportunity to do something kind for someone." This creates feelings of good will and promotes gratitude in your own life.

You can cultivate feelings of gratitude about your life and the beautiful amazing attributes of your world. Just *stop* and take the moment required to *look*. This is so easy and transformative; all you really have to do is "walk the walk." All you have to do is take an awareness moment as often as possible throughout your day when pick out the truly amazing things you love about your life.

MONEY IS MIND
OVER MATTER

I would like you to set aside what you currently believe to be true about money. I say this because most people have many perspectives that are so self-inhibiting that letting in any new information on this topic is very difficult for them. If you're like me, you have read several books on the subject and much advice on how to get money, save it, and invest it. That information is plentiful and useful, but that's not what we are going to be talking about here.

Mental perspectives on money can be very different for each person and greatly depend on how a person was brought up. A child brought up in a poor household sees mostly the issues and obstacles surrounding the topic of money. A poor child can form a perspective that instills defeat or one that drives him or her to overcome the obstacles at any cost. And a middle-class child will often be motivated to earn a middle-class income.

It is said that money in itself is an effect of a successful endeavor, and money cannot be sought after directly. Consider that there is a mental process that can unblock your inhibitions and make the process of getting money much easier.

We all need it to pay bills, buy food, and give ourselves and family the material items and freedom we think we deserve. Most people gauge how well they are doing in life by the amount of money they make. People's anxieties about money can be extreme to none at all.

These anxieties are not just for the poor; people who have large amounts of money at risk lose sleep over their cache of wealth. We all have different comfort levels when it comes to our mental state regarding risk. If you are ever going to be comfortable about the topic of money, you need to step back your debt and investment risk to the point that you are at ease.

When your thoughts focus on a lack of money for whatever reason, it creates a negative feeling that prevents your mental connection to more. When you worry about your job, your mortgage payment, or any other aspect of money, you hold your mind in a state of disease or unrest. Only you know your comfort level and what the right amount of debt or risk for you.

You have two choices regarding clearing your negative feelings, thoughts, and anxieties. Do the mental work to become comfortable with money in your current situation or reduce your debt and risk to the point where you are at ease with your financial picture.

Believe with all of your
heart that you will do what
you were made to do.

—Orison Swett Marden

HOW DO YOU *REALLY* FEEL ABOUT MONEY

How you really feel about money is a direct indication of your beliefs about money, conscious and subconscious. You are living the results of your beliefs currently. If you believe in prosperity and abundance regarding money and material items, that will be evident in your current reality.

If you believe that life is hard and money only comes to you through struggle, that will be the reality for you. Where most people seem to struggle is in the emotional connection to prosperity. You must feel financial abundance and good fortune in order for your mental inhibitions to melt away. Often, emotional scars and influences from our impressionable years hold us back.

If you really want to change your current reality, you need to leave behind all the emotional baggage from your past and focus solely on the good feelings and emotions that your future prosperity will bring. *Impressing good thoughts continuously into your current reality modifies your current beliefs and changes your future.* Your current mental state is greatly influenced by your thoughts or "mind talk";

what you're telling yourself is either reinforcing your current reality or it is reshaping your reality for a new and improved future.

QUIZ
IDENTIFYING NEGATIVE
BELIEFS ABOUT MONEY

On a scale of 1 to 10, how positive do you feel regarding money?

Rate each question and total your score independently for parts 1 and 2.

10 I strongly agree.
 7 I agree.
 5 I am neutral.
 3 I disagree.
 0 I strongly disagree.

Remember to really think about your answers and be as honest as possible to get an accurate result.

Part 1: Getting and Saving Money

1. For me, money is easy to come by.
2. I enjoy spending money.
3. I rarely worry about money.
4. Money flows in and out of my life.
5. My life is too short to worry about money.
6. I always have enough money to be comfortable.

7. Saving money is not difficult.
8. I enjoy watching my savings grow.
9. I can spend my savings whenever I like.
10. I feel lucky to have the income I currently have.

Part 2: Negative Thoughts about Money

1. For me, money is difficult to come by.
2. I do not enjoy spending money.
3. When I have a pile of cash in my hand, I feel nervous.
4. Everyone else gets more money than me.
5. Everything is going up except my income.
6. Money holds me back from everything I want.
7. Saving money is difficult.
8. I really hate spending my savings.
9. I purchase lottery tickets but rarely win.
10. I absolutely need to find a way to create more income.

Assessing your score

Add up your score for part 1 and 2 separately, so you will have a positive and a negative score.

In this scale it is easy to see which way you are leaning and where you need to shift your focus more to the positive side.

Positive Score

100 to 51

Congratulations on your high score and your positive beliefs regarding money and prosperity. Your score is likely directly reflected in your lifestyle and material possessions. Your perspective has likely been a long-term work, which has benefitted you greatly. Money for you is an effect of positive linear thinking and flows from the many met goals. Naturally you look forward to success each day. If for some reason things do not work out as planned, this seems foreign to you, as you have come to expect the best and you know that in the end everything will work out.

50 or less

Your perspective toward money is skewed and requires your attention if you truly desire change. I recommend you use the *double-up challenge* to free you from insecurity or inhibitions regarding money. When you feel guarded or at risk because of money, you are putting up mental blocks that prohibit the flow. You cannot feel the pinch or restrictive feelings associated with the lack of money. If you truly desire more money to flow through your life, apply mind-over-matter thinking every day.

Negative Score

0 to 25

When you score over 50 on the positive side and less than 25 on the negative side, this is a balanced score. If you scored less than 15, you are doing exceptionally well. We all have some misgivings about money at one time or another; we must all learn from our mistakes and find out what works best. Money is a mind game that can have deep emotional roots. Being able to let go and think positively about future events allows you to be unencumbered by emotions and negative thoughts holding you back from your success.

26 or more

When you score 50 or less on the positive side and more than 26 on the negative, it means there is an imbalance. You have to want to make changes and to understand that it will take at least thirty days before your new habits will stick. If you want a beautiful garden, you have to plan your work and work your plan. If you do not follow through, the garden will simply default back to the original plot of soil, as if nothing had taken place at all.

CLEAR VISION AND DETERMINATION

It is always amazing to me to see how an immigrant can come to this country with no more than a shirt on his or her back and set onto a path of wealth in very short order. Often these people are coming from a land of oppression and discovering freedom for the very first time. In no time at all, they get to work on their priorities, often working for years on minimum wage, collecting and saving every nickel until they are able to go into business for themselves. It is not uncommon to see them with two or more jobs and supporting family back home.

In most cases, clear focus and determination have been manifesting in their minds or for as long as they can remember. The dream of being free to pursue a lifestyle of freedom and growth is so entrenched in their minds that success is imminent if given the opportunity. These individuals often use every resource to cut costs and be successful.

Determination and a sense of purpose are often instilled at a very young age. A burning desire puts these young people directly on the path to seeking opportunity at any personal cost. Clearly the conditioning of their minds is the driving force to success. They do not believe in failure, and they are in no way whimsical, complacent, or happy with the status quo.

There is a big difference between wishful thinking and committed thinking. Your mind and subconscious mind are totally impressionable. It is true that you can have, be, or do anything. All you have to do is want it badly enough and for a long enough time to change your beliefs. Remember, a belief is only a series of thoughts you keep thinking.

Interestingly, children raised in middle-income families, who have their needs met, will often opt for a middle-income lifestyle and education. The mind-over-matter determination process is not present in them as it is in many impoverish children and immigrants.

We all want success and money, but how motivated are we to seek change? It depends on our willingness to change our beliefs. We all have the tools, but many have chosen to believe that the desired changes are not possible for them. Rising above self-imposed metal restrictions can take time, but it cannot happen if the desire for change is not present.

Inducing change without changing your beliefs causes you to default to previous scenarios regarding previous conditions. When you take your beliefs with you, there is very little or no induced change beyond the immediate action process. True change happens when you move past old belief systems into new thought patterns. Employing new thoughts of gratitude and acceptance is needed in the pursuit of a worthy goal; they allow mental blocks and inhibitions to fall away and be left behind.

Using the positive aspects process can help you identify areas of negativity and can circumvent problematic patterns. Mind-over- matter processes are not new but have been used unknowingly for thousands of years. Marking and rereading this book often and applying the processes and principles provided will change your life. As always, it is up to you to desire change.

> Life is like riding a bicycle.
> To keep your balance, you
> must keep moving.
> —Albert Einstein

CHANGING YOUR PERSPECTIVE REGARDING MONEY

When you change your self-talk and conversations about money from negative to positive, it opens doors and possibilities that you would not otherwise have seen. Changing your beliefs about money happens slowly with attention to the words in your head and coming from your mouth. As you change your attitude and then your beliefs about money, it brings relief, reduces stress, keeps you healthier, and lets you enjoy life more.

When you believe that your life is full of opportunity and freedom, that is what opens the doors to happiness and prosperity.

"

Once you understand what is
causing a change or a lack
of change, you are able to
take control of your money
and success in your life.

"

CHANGING YOUR
SELF-TALK ABOUT MONEY

Mental preparation regarding money is very similar to the work needed for goals and success. Pay attention to what you are saying out loud to others and yourself. If you are like most people, you need to shift you thinking from negative to positive in order to remove your self-imposed limitations.

Bringing more money into your awareness may require a transition from past tense into your now or present tense. When you project thoughts about your future, it is not the same as applying the thought or perspective change to your current reality or your now. In other words, all power is now; as you push the changes into your future, you are setting yourself up for change, but not necessarily applying the changes until you actually believe the new thought to be true for you.

It is totally understandable that most people cannot shift their beliefs instantly; it takes time to change your current mind-set. The list below is given as an example. Feel free to modify the words or context to suit your current situation or mental disposition.

Negative self-talk	Positive self-talk
• I never have enough.	I always get by.
• I'll be happy when ...	I'm happy now; I get more.
• I could never get ahead.	I'm doing better than most people.
• Why can't I get more?	I always get what I need.
• I wish I had more money.	Money and opportunity are coming.
• Four more years until my raise.	My hobby can bring in extra cash.
• I'm not lucky with investments.	Low-risk investments work for me.
• I am always behind.	I'm going to rent out my unused room.
• The government is to blame.	I like reading about success stories.
• Money is hard to get.	My understanding of money is evolving.
• How can I ever get enough?	I like to see what others are doing for extra income.

> Every day is a journey, and
> the journey itself is home.
>
> —Bashô,, *Narrow Road to the Interior*

THIS IS WHAT IS
HOLDING YOU BACK

Your thoughts, emotions, and beliefs can be viewed as three parts of the same process.

1. Think of your beliefs as the foundation of known reality on which your thoughts and responses are based.
2. Consider your thoughts as the data processing you conduct to determine if dialogues and situations match up with your beliefs about your world.
3. Think of your mentally stored emotions as your mentally stored sensory perception, which has lightning-fast speed that can tell you in a heartbeat what you should be thinking or acting on at that moment.

When you make a conscience effort through awareness to work with and modify stored mental conditions, it makes grassroots changes in who you are and perpetuates progress into things you want in your life. *You are making positive progress toward an improved mental state and improved reality when you feel positive emotion toward a specifi c topic.*

If you can create only limited positive feelings about a topic, it is a strong indication that your beliefs require work or modification into a more positive receptive state. *It can be very difficult to move forward with physical action if you believe openly or even subconsciously that the end result is not possible.* For example, if you believe that the process of saving money will be difficult or impossible, at least at some level, you are definitely going to have difficulty attaining your savings goals.

Are these or similar thoughts a part of your thoughts about a desired change?

- I can't because...
- I wish I could...
- I never...
- I was born that way.
- It only happens to other people.
- This is my reality.
- This is the way things are.
- I'm stuck in this situation.
- It's someone else's (or something else's) fault.
- I wish I had more money.
- I wish I was rich.
- Someday I will...

Shifting your conditioned mind-set from focusing on lacking what you want to focusing on a goal, desired change, or end result is how you get exactly what you want.

You cannot move forward with permanent changes until you believe you can.

"

To acquire true self power
you have to feel beneath
no one, be immune to
criticism and be fearless.

—Deepak Chopra

"

MAKE A MENTAL CONNECTION TO YOUR PROSPERITY

For many people, it may seem difficult or nearly impossible to make a mental connection to personal prosperity. Beliefs and conditioning run deep in our culture, and deep-rooted feelings create barriers for many, as money has been seen as a measure of worth or stature.

The lines between the lower middle and upper classes were clearly drawn in the mud in the fifties or earlier. When you look at working-class families in the metropolitan areas of North America, you can see that there has been a steady decrease in the segregation between the classes due to the information age and the availability of money.

When you talk with someone from the generation that worked in the forties and fifties, wages of less than two dollars per day were not uncommon. Most people were struggling to compete, and a college or university education was for the rich, elite, and fortunate. For the most part, the majority of the labor force was unskilled, and competition for labor jobs was fierce.

Since money now moves around electronically, the working class has been able to find long-term stability. In general, economies have been able to self-perpetuate. In the space of one generation we have seen the availability of money grow to the point where there is finally plenty to go around for the majority of the North American population.

From a monetary and opportunistic perspective, most of us have never been in a better position to prosper.

Connecting to your personal potential and your opportunities as an individual is very important, as it connects you with positive feelings about growth. When you believe that there is a world of opportunity just waiting for you, you open your mind, and positive emotions help you to gravitate to what you feel best about. If you believe you are restricted and limited, that will be your reality until you change it. We are amazing creatures endowed and blessed with a world so diverse and so rich in resources, it honors and humbles me to be a part of it.

Make no mistake; no matter who you are, if you still have some years ahead of you, you are standing on the threshold of the hyper-expansion of the human species. Your potential for growth and prosperity has never been greater. All you have to do is mentally align with your desires and pursue your dream with all your heart.

"

Be thankful for what you
have; you'll end up having
more. If you concentrate on
what you don't have, you will
never, ever have enough.

—Oprah Winfrey

"

THIRTY-DAY CHALLENGE: MENTALLY FREE UP YOUR MONEY

We are creatures of habit or repetition. We thrive on routine, which provides comfort and security and allows us a stable environment to raise a family or retire. Repetition allows us to relax into a predictable comfort zone, where limiting thoughts allows us to cruise through a given task or routine. This routine is the self-limiting mind-set that creates barriers that hold you within that comfort zone. When you buy something, do you feel apprehension? Do you spend money in a guarded fashion? This mental disposition is a self-inhibiting state that prevents you from connecting to the flow of money or abundance. Like your goals, unless you connect with the desired result in a positive fashion, you are holding yourself apart from the things you desire.

Creating new patterns of thoughts and enjoying abundance on a small scale opens your receptivity to bigger things for you in the future. Purchasing items mentally is an exercise that starts the transition into mentally accepting the flow of money. Enjoying spending money mentally changes your perspective about what is acceptable and possible for you.

When you consider the amount of time you have spent affirming your current thoughts, it is easy to see why your mind is firmly set in its current patterns.

Here is an example of freeing up your mental conditioned thoughts. Go to a luxury car dealership and sit in one of the beautiful showroom cars for a time. Connect with a higher belief that these things are tangible for you. You really just need to shift your thoughts and desires about what is important and for you. You have to manifest the desire, fall in love with the concept, and be willing to explore all the avenues to bring this about.

If for some reason you cannot consider such an action, you need to transition into the process of having and spending money more slowly.

To bring about a shift from our standard repetitive comfort zone, we need to phase in a new repetitive action until it becomes a default action in our minds.

The thirty-day challenge is designed to do just that. The process is designed to be repetitive enough that it shifts your default thoughts and removes apprehension and anxieties regarding spending money. Remember, to let money in, you have to change your feelings and perspectives regarding money.

To complete this challenge, you are going to mentally spend $45,000. In the left column is the amount of money you need to spend today. Go online or pick out items you would like to have if the money was real.

The rules are simple: one transaction per day; no more than three duplicate items on the entire list; and items must reasonably reflect the amount of money spent. Use any source to find items to buy mentally. If you miss one or two days, just pick up where you left off. Do not try to catch up or blitz the list, as this defeats the purpose.

Connecting with having these items and enjoying the purchase with a sense of satisfaction anchors the experience.

Abundance is not
something we acquire.
It is something we tune into.

—Wayne Dyer

#	$	Items Purchased
1	100.	3 NEW DVDs
2	200.	New espresso machine
3	300.	
4	400.	
5	500.	
6	600.	
7	700.	
8	800.	
9	900.	
10	1,000.	
11	1,100.	
12	1,200.	
13	1,300.	
14	1,400.	
15	1,500.	
16	1,600.	
17	1,700.	
18	1,800.	
19	1,900.	
20	2,000.	
21	2,100.	
22	2,200.	
23	2,300.	
24	2,400.	
25	2,500.	
26	2,600.	
27	2,700.	
28	2,800.	
29	2,900.	
30	3,000.	

OPEN YOUR MIND TO INTUITIVE PERCEPTION

There is a lot of misconception regarding the word *meditation*. *Meditation* is interchangeable with *contemplation*. In my experience a meditation is simply a means of giving your mind the opportunity to see the fragments of information you may have otherwise missed or could not perceive regarding desired results. Connecting with or allowing information to flow from your higher mind is simple and a very natural state.

Self-disciplines can be taken to some substantial extremes; I think that the Japanese have demonstrated this better than any other culture, with their discipline in martial arts and religious practices.

You already meditate while performing repetitive tasks that you enjoy and you do not notice the passage of time. This mental connection can be an intuitive or perceptive mental process where you connect with your higher mind or subconscious mind and gain wonderful insights or ideas regarding the topic you are pondering at that time. Think of some daily, repetitive activities that you perform on a regular basis, such as mowing the lawn or driving for extended periods. Other examples include knitting, doing hobbies, walking, running—basically anything that allows your mind to relax. These spaces of time can be very useful to you if your intent is focusing on a desired result or goal.

Meditation, or contemplation, has been used effectively for centuries by many religious figures to hone in on the finer aspects of the human mind. Using this highly effective tool is much simpler more and effective than you may think; it does not have to involve certain postures or uncomfortable positions.

The fact is most of us already use forms of meditation daily. When you understand that your mind is a recording device and what you put in is what you get out, you begin to understand why meditation is a very useful tool in the mind-over-matter processes.

Chances are you already know or have connected with a very useful piece of information regarding a topic that is already on your mind. Allow the time and space to connect with the rest of it. In my experience, the best intuitive information has come forward in this manner. Many of the insights and concepts for this book were brought about through this process.

I highly recommend using quiet moments in the early hours of the day. This is when you mind is free of action and media-related information. It also allows time and space to bring invaluable insight you may not otherwise have access too.

Get a fresh piece of paper and sit in a comfortable, quiet spot—with a cup of coffee, if you like. This will allow you time to reflect on any topic you wish. You may be amazed with the information that comes forth.

"

There is no scarcity of opportunity
to make a living at what you
love; there's only scarcity of
resolve to make it happen.

—Wayne Dyer

"

SAY IT UNTIL
YOU BELIEVE IT

Contemplation or meditation is an ideal way to reinforce a new desired reality. You cannot attain the goals or things you want until you believe you can. Your beliefs most often are the one thing keeping you apart from your new and improved reality. To reinforce change, you must get used to the idea or concept through a repetitive, cumulative bonding process with your end point. Part of the goal is mentally connecting with the benefits of the desired goal. Helping your mind secure beliefs regarding the desired result and anchoring the thoughts with positive emotion can be done with a joyful meditative process.

Think of meditation as an enjoyable daydream or mental video where you get to feel amazing. Make it a point each time to make it better and more real. This exercise has kept me up at night, so I suggest utilizing any time except bedtime. Pick a quiet spot without interruption where relaxation is possible. Otherwise use the time when joyful hobbies or exercise are happening.

Post pictures from any source to remind you to repeat this process, such as on a treadmill or lawn tractor.

Perform this process as often as possible in the beginning. By reinforcing the desired result in your subconscious mind, you gradually record over your doubts. Positive thoughts soon start to spill out into your reality, causing all kinds of wonderful changes. *Say and think your positive thoughts over and over until you believe them.*

"

It's never crowded along
the extra mile.

—Wayne Dyer

"

DEALING WITH RESISTANCE

When positive changes start to happen, there can be some resistance to change, especially from spouses or people close to you. They will not recognize the pattern, and not knowing what is happening with you can cause some concern. Offering gentle, uplifting advice is the key to offsetting resistance. Sometimes moving slower in terms of changes that involve others or confiding in someone who is more open minded is a short-term solution.

Contemplation

I have included some ideas regarding the contemplation process. Your contemplation or meditation process can consist of any worthwhile goal that stirs your emotions. Write out your ideal end-point scenario and build on it, revel in it; pack joy and tears of emotion into this process. When you are ready and start the action process, it's like gravity itself drawing through the sequence of events. Contemplate, build, and believe your dream goal. It's why you're here in this world in the first place!

A SPORTS GOAL CONTEMPLATION

I am so proud of the fact that winning is totally attainable for me. I am at one with the physical movements. I move with precision and ease as I focus through the finish line. My body excels to a level beyond all others. It is joy, harmony, symmetry, exhalation, and raw power in motion. I am totally excited and motivated to reach my pinnacle by standing on the podium with my gold metal. The thought of my victory is so sweet.

My heart races each time I hear the roar of the crowd and see the flash of the cameras. In the final moments of the competition, the adrenaline is pumping and sweat is flying. The moment for euphoria is explosively upon me. The elation and physical exertion is beyond measure. It is what I live for!

"

You miss 100 percent of the
shots you never take.

—Wayne Gretzky

"

A MONEY CONTEMPLATION

I love knowing that as I add joy and positive emotion to the subject of money, it opens doors and allows me to move closer to having what I want. I love knowing that a sea of money is always flowing and can flow through my hands if I allow it. As I allow money to flow through me, it creates freedom and releases me into the lifestyle I desire. It feels so good to be in this position; it removes all stress and worry and replaces them with joy.

As I enjoy my money, it enables me to travel, eat, and drink in some of the most beautiful places in the world. The food, the wine, and the sunsets are so glorious that my eyes well up with the profound beauty. As I enjoy my money and freedom, I gather friends and family in the most joyous locations.

My money allows me clothes that are made from the finest, most comfortable materials. I love the smell of the Italian leather in the many sports cars available to me. I love knowing that I can help people in need make lasting changes.

Capital isn't scarce; vision is.

—Sam Walton

A BUSINESS CONTEMPLATION

Our business goal is totally exciting. I love the exhilaration of the end point. The synergy is like electricity in the air. My heartbeat picks up when I think about us in the winner's circle, receiving the recognition we so deserve. Our focus on details and fortitude is second to none; we have a winning combination and a clear advantage over all competitors. I can see the end point clearly, and as the culmination of events unfolds, the excitement level builds to a fever pitch. We are so fortunate to be on the cutting edge of this technology, because it catapults us into amazing exponential opportunities. I love this and can't wait to get to the next step.

There are only two ways
to live your life.
One is as though nothing
is a miracle.
The other is as though
everything is a miracle.

—Albert Einstein

REST, DIET, AND EXERCISE TO POWER AND BALANCE YOUR MIND

Success is also found in our personal capacity to excel on a daily, ongoing basis. If something is out of balance, we are inhibiting our chance of succeeding over the long term. Most of us take our mind for granted, forgetting that we are the keepers of a highly complex, evolving, biological nerve center firing off electrical signals millions of times per second to billons of neurons during every active moment of our lives. This circuitry has a fragile balance greatly influenced by self-imposed conditions. For example, most people don't realize they have a choice when facing negative emotions that are either self-imposed or from outside influences. Frustration due to stress is manageable under normal conditions and with a little effort can be defused or completely avoided.

Some body management issues can lead to ongoing personal problems, most of which can be resolved through rest, diet, and exercise. Everyone needs eight hours of sleep, whether they think they do or not, and a lack of rest can lead to disorders if not properly managed. Rest actually de-stresses you, keeping your mind alert and functioning properly.

Diet is something very few people pay attention to, but some foods do have a negative effect on metabolism and the mind. Limiting animal fats and highly processed foods can cause a big change when replaced with foods that give you energy. Vitamin B supplements can calm most people, taking away that edgy feeling. Reducing coffee intake or replacing coffee with green tea will decrease your caffeine dependency, eliminating the rock-bottom feeling as the caffeine wears off.

Exercise is what your body needs to maintain good posture and good overall mental health. Vascular health is everything to your brain; keeping your blood flowing puts oxygen and nutrients to where they are needed most. Letting your body go without some form of activity is like letting your car go until the engine light comes on—and often that is too late. If you let your muscles wither until you are a regular customer to a chiropractor, its time you made a decision about what you would rather have—exercise or chronic back pain.

Of course, there are always exceptions, but don't be a victim of your personal excuses. For most of us, the writing is on the wall. The sustainability and longevity of the human mind is really in the hands of the owner occupant. By giving attention to your mental health and physical maintenance, you are investing in your success.

"

He who controls others may
be powerful, but he who has
mastered himself is mightier still.

—Lao Tzu

"

You are the only one who can make a big difference for you; you can phase in lifestyle changes that can be a powerful catalyst to other changes. Improving your life is just mind over matter as you take control of you.

Ten ways to get better rest

Getting enough sleep and sleeping well are known to boost cognitive function. Your performance on any day greatly depends on how well you slept the night before. Here are a few personal rules to adopt to keep you on track for a great night's sleep.

1. Get exercise. You cannot sleep well if your body has pent-up energy. Any physical activity helps. Here is one good rule of thumb: break sweat at least once a day. It really doesn't matter what the activity is. Your body is a highly effective, calorie-burning machine; it needs to move and burn the fuel you consume every day.

2. Empty your mind. You cannot rest well if you go to bed with your mind working on the concerns of the day, on getting ready for tomorrow, or

on any other mental activity that requires your attention. A busy mind will prevent a good rest. Make a point of allowing wind-down time, such as reading uplifting material in bed. This allows your body and mind to cycle down. Avoid any material that will cause stress or put your mind into an active sequence.

3. Eating before bed, (yes, we all have done it) or going to bed on a full stomach can cause internal discomfort and excessive dreaming. The REM (rapid eye movement) state is the deep, restful sleep we all wish for. There is a reason why doctors and health nutritionists recommend that the largest meal of the day be lunch, allowing time for digestion, which for most people is more effective when they're active. Plan that big turkey feast for three in the afternoon and following up with any activity will allow everyone the opportunity for a good night's rest. Busy families can utilize a slow cooker for earlier meals. The general rule is to eat dinner earlier whenever possible.

4. Reduce caffeine intake early in the day, as caffeine is known to affect most people up to ten hours after consumption. Herbal teas can bridge the gap in the evenings.

5. Our kids are wired in more ways than one before bed. Removing electronics from the bedroom is necessary to allow their minds time wind down, which will never happen if they are not getting enough activity or have

consumed sweets before bed. I often talk to my boys about balance and cause and effect. When they get an understanding of the why, I ask them what would be the better choice, and they often comply willingly. Even mature teens need help removing their phones from their bedrooms due to late-night texting and need to be managed to prevent poor mental performance the next day due to lack of sleep.

6. Take time to set yourself up for the best sleep possible. Make sure your bed is comfortable. Down duvets, firm beds, and flat pillows are generally best for the long haul. If you learn to cherish your sleep time and have fresh sheets, it can be something to really look forward to.

7. Do not turn your bed into an office for texts, phone calls, making lists, or watching TV. Your sleep should be predicated on relaxation not exhaustion.

8. Keep your bedroom cool and quiet whenever possible, making sure others in the household follow a designated quiet time. I recommend giving fair warning to avoid protests. Use blinds and ceiling fans to keep rooms cool and dark. Moving into the basement during the hot summer months is a common alternative to sleeping in upper-floor bedrooms—particularly those on a south or west wall.

9. Use night-lights in bedrooms and hallways to prevent completely waking up during a trip to the bathroom.

10. Take naps during the day to recover lost sleep. It is truly amazing what a ten-minute power nap can do to revive you during a busy day. Pulling off the road into a rest area or park for ten minutes can be more effective than a cup of coffee. Consider slipping out to your vehicle for a lunch break and setting your cell phone alarm.

Consume more EFAs and almonds

In my years of research and adjustments to my diet, I have made many discoveries. I want to share what I feel is the best advice possible, but keep in mind that professional advice from a qualified nutritionist is invaluable. Most of us are well aware of the many benefits of essential fatty acids, or EFAs. According to Dr. Rudy Siva, our brain is up to 50 percent good fat content by weight and at least 20 percent of that comes from EPA and DHA oils. His recommendations for a healthier brain include the following:

1. Eat fish at least once a week.
2. Introduce olive oil and flaxseed oils into your diet.
3. Eat more nuts, especially almonds, which are believed to improve memory. Drinking almond milk, which is made from crushed almond nuts, is an easy way to up your EFA intake.

Switch from sugar to honey

Most heath experts consider sugar to be a nonfood. Excess sugar is known to cause claustrophobia, memory loss, and other neurotic disorders. Honey is a natural sweetener that is a healthy sugar replacement; it provides natural calories and energy for your body.

Honey can boost your immune system and satisfy your body's need for sweets.

Detoxify and fast for a day

Fasting cleans and detoxifies our bodies. We tax our bodies by eating every single day. If you think about, in nature that is a very unnatural state for any mammal. Toxins and processed foods cause stress on our digestive system, but also can drain our brain capacity and energy. Fasting allows the organs in the body time to catch up, and it can help improve metal clarity, memory, and concentration.

Eat avocados

According to Ann Kulze, MD, author of *Dr. Ann's 10-Step Diet*, avocados are known as "the fatty fruit." They contain monounsaturated fat, which contributes to healthy blood flow. "And healthy blood flow means a healthy brain," she says. Avocados also lower blood pressure, according to Kulze. And as hypertension is a risk factor for the decline in cognitive abilities; lower blood pressure promotes brain health. Avocados are high in calories, however, so Kulze suggests adding just a quarter to a half an avocado to one daily meal as a side dish.

Take multivitamins and vitamin B-complex

Multivitamins have been proven to improve energy and cognitive function. Improved clarity and memory are direct benefits from taking daily multivitamin supplements.

Vitamin B-complex has been shown to improve cognitive memory. Eating foods high in vitamin B-complex is easy; beef, tuna, oats, turkey, Brazil nuts, bananas, potatoes, avocados, and legumes all contain it.

Most nutritionists agree that it's best to stay away from or limit high- starch foods and bleached white flour, which deplete the vitamin B-complex necessary for a healthy mind.

"

You only live once, but if you
do it right, once is enough.

—Mae West

"

DEFINE YOURSELF
FOR YOURSELF

In this often-crowded, unforgiving world, it can be difficult to gain a proper perspective on a secure, fulfilling future. Remaining true to yourself is the first and most basic fundamental. Not all of us have had the life-influencing benefit of a good role model. Life has a way of teaching lessons that can't be forgotten. Peer pressure and poor environments can be a catalyst for disastrous consequences. Identifying with core values can be the difference between having or not having a successful future where trust is required. This is why many business partnerships often fail. If one or more of the partners do not have the integrity to be honest and forthright with business and personal information, the partnership is at risk of failure. Having high personal moral standards and recognizing a poor track record regarding performance or behavior at someone else's expense should be on every person's mind when considering a partnership.

Walking away from poor or high-risk circumstances with people who lack personal integrity will boost you above a morally deficient group. When examining a group of friends, look at their track record of accomplishments and of trouble. Typically a group will perpetuate more of the same based on existing values and leadership.

Identifying with a person or organization that has amazing accomplishments or finding like-minded individuals with integrity and aspirations is the way to put your future on track.

"

The greatest and glorious
masterpiece of man is to know
how to live to purpose.

—Michel de Montaigne

"

Success for most of us is simply getting and having what we want. When you break it down for most people, success can be as simple as a joyful life. Material items do not offer lasting gratification. Joyously sharing time with others offers the best memories. All you have do is look at your personal photographs to confirm this.

Money can provide more choices and more freedom. Lasting happiness comes from within, so deciding today that you are going to enjoy what you have here and now creates a feeling of success and happiness. This in turn opens up your mind to improved scenarios. Happiness and lasting success come from within, but you have to want it bad enough to commit to change. Statements starting with "I'll be happy when ..." push your success into the future, but it can never be yours if you do not bring it into your now.

If you can't get up the motivation and commit to change, you are accepting what is currently in your reality as what you want. For some people, defining what they want is difficult, due to lack of perspective. Envisioning a goal is work, and you really do have to work at it. So build the details and emotions until you savor the goal and go there often. Your mind is the pathway to having an improved situation—for any situation.

When you say, "This is my reality," you reinforce the now as unchangeable. If you are completely happy with that, great! But if you are not, then you have work to do. Define, refine, add emotional attachments, and implement changes. You will be successful only at what you mentally allow yourself to be. True long-term success is a self-imposed mental state.

The sooner you dial in your focus on what you want and accept and believe that what you want is yours, the sooner you will be enjoying what is naturally yours.

"

Go for it now.
The future is promised to no one.

—Wayne Dyer

"

FINAL WORDS

Find the inspiration to keep yourself mentally on track day by day. Post pictures of your goals and write down the reasons that motivate you. Expose yourself to inspiring and motivating slogans, stories, and literature. Set your goals for your standard of living as high as you possibly can, and be willing to push them higher. Always reach for feelings of well-being and gratitude. Be thankful for the blessings in your life. As you connect to these things and hold them with positive emotion, you gravitate mentally and physically into that reality.

> "People often say that motivation doesn't last. Well, neither does bathing—that's why we recommend it daily."
>
> —Zig Ziglar

I AM

CARING

STRONG

HEALTHY

ABUNDANT

ENTHUSIASTIC

RADIANT

LOVING

APPRECIATIVE

PEACEFUL

I AM A WILLING STUDENT OF LIFE AND ALL
THAT IS I AM BETTER THAN I USED TO BE

I AM